The Invocation of Presence

by E.J. Gold

The Invocation of Presence

by E.J. Gold

Gateways Books and Tapes
PO Box 370, Nevada City, Ca. 95959
530-271-2239

The Invocation of Presence
by E.J. Gold

Published in a Private Edition by: Gateways Books and Tapes
P.O. Box 370 Nevada City, CA 95959-0370
ph: (530) 271-2239 or (800) 869-0658
email: info@gatewaysbooksandtapes.com

http://www.idhhb.com http://www.gatewaysbooksandtapes.com
ISBN Softcover: 978-0-89556-075-9
ISBN PDF: 978-0-89556-659-1
ISBN Kindle: 978-0-89556-660-7
ISBN Epub: 978-0-89556-661-4
ISBN Mobi: 978-0-89556-662-1

Library of Congress Cataloging-in-Publication Data

Names: Gold, E. J., author.
Title: The invocation of presence / by E.J. Gold.
Description: Nevada City, Ca. : Gateways Books and Tapes, [2021] |
Summary:

"Beginning with a question to the reader on "The Key to Life," author
E.J. Gold presents a conversational introduction to his highly
recommended, most basic meditation and self-study exercise, the
invocation of presence. This is a simple and lucid exercise to apply in
everyday life, any time, anywhere--which does not mean it is an easy
practice to maintain. In this step by step tutorial, Gold asks the
reader for no philosophy, no religion, no particular belief system at
all--only the willingness of the reader or student of inner work to
experiment with the practice and collect one's own personal impressions
and insights from it"-- Provided by publisher.

Identifiers: LCCN 2021028128 (print) | LCCN 2021028129 (ebook) | ISBN
9780895560759 (softcover) | ISBN 9780895566591 (pdf)
Subjects: LCSH: Spirituality. | Spiritual life. | Meditation. |
Life--Miscellanea.
Classification: LCC BF1999 .G62164 2021 (print) | LCC BF1999 (ebook) |
DDC 204/.35--dc23
LC record available at https://lccn.loc.gov/2021028128
LC ebook record available at https://lccn.loc.gov/2021028129

TABLE OF CONTENTS

KEY TO LIFE

"At the end of your life, if you do nothing to prepare for it, you will find yourself struggling for another day, another hour, another minute, just another breath.

"This is what ordinary phenomenal life is all about. It is a fixation on survival into the future, but how can this be, without voluntary participation in the present?

"Even if you have accomplished the greatest thing in the world, if you penetrate with your vision fifty million years into the future and then look back on your life and ask what you have accomplished, you will see what it really means to be alive.

"What could you have accomplished fifty million years ago that would mean anything now? This is the question that reveals the only real mystery of life, and anyone who possesses an authentic answer to this question holds the key to life itself."

WHY WORK ON OURSELVES AT ALL?

1.   We have all had glimpses of something beyond phenomenal-organic reality. We remember these glimpses.

2.   We feel drawn to this non-phenomenal vision of reality.

3.   We have made individual efforts and they have failed.

4.   We are completely disappointed in the organic world and its achievements, and the loss of everything when at the end of life, we are swept away by forces beyond our control.

5.   We have experienced the necessity for correctly organized group effort.

6.   The group effort supports a special unique type of consciousness which can eventually, through repetition and voluntary establishment of exalted habits, be aligned to the Work.

7.   We are shipwrecked among people who are wholly absorbed in the mechanical pursuits of organic life. In a group, we find for the first time others with whom we can share our ideas, lives and experiences. Here, in the work-community, it is permitted to be authentic.

8.   We are running out of time. Every available moment must be used for work.

9.   Work on self, establishing the attention and presence of one's

rightful I, by self-invocation, and the study of the machine, to form a bridge between organic life and the Work.

10. Group discipline is a constant reminder of our work to take our place in the circle of invocation.

11. The voluntary work program makes possible the use of ordinary actions of daily life for the Work, with inner exercises, producing alchemical transformation to the non-phenomenal real world.

12. The voluntary work program is designed to produce automatic habitual conditioning for conscious passage through the phenomenal world and rebirth into the non-phenomenal world.

13. The active study of the machine, combined with activation of presence, clarifies one's vision of the non-phenomenal reality.

14. Work on self provides a special situation in which individuals can confront and produce voluntarily those factors which have been a problem for them in the eternal, non-phenomenal world.

HERE I AM

G. "held court" at the Tiptoe Inn, a fabulous bakery and delicatessen on the north side of Broadway near the Ansonia Hotel where he had been staying in Mrs. C.'s apartment, and several new pupils decided to offer him a ride around Manhattan, north on FDR Drive, across Harlem and down on the Hudson River Drive back to his "office".

It began calmly enough, but then G. insisted that he drive the car, a large, expensive Bentley open coupe.

His driving skills and daredevil driving were well-known by all the members of the groups. He wasn't exactly reckless, but one had the impression that he was trying to stay on a brahma bull that had run amok.

It was hard to remember in all this that he actually had control of the car. It seemed to us that the car had a mind of its own, which G. was barely able to reason with, and which required his constant dramatic over-corrections.

As we drove up the FDR parkway, G. began to speak . . .

"Here I am! In this wonderful machine . . . !

"And my own organic machine, meanwhile, is receiving and categorizing impressions, in response to which my marvelous head-brain, without which I would be completely and utterly ignorant and unable to orient myself, happens to think categorically in more or less random patterns of association, whether real or imagined, in response to the general patterns of impressions . . .

" . . . and here I am, having a fascinating conversation with myself, an inner dialogue which, if it were only able to be recorded for posterity, would, without doubt, become the classic philosophical reasoning posture for all future generations to come on the subject of . . .

" . . . but what was it I was just a moment ago thinking about?

". . . it all seemed so lucid. I understood something about something which I had never understood before and which, unless I am mistaken, has never yet been really formulated quite so clearly by anyone else . . .

" . . . it's so difficult to try to remember what it was that seemed so clear a moment ago while my organic machine is forced to bumble and fidget in more or less spasmodic reflex, responding automatically and semi-automatically to a combination of inner and outer events and influences, both real and imaginary, putt-putting along like this beautiful new automobile, with more or less the same mechanical smoothness.

" . . . unless, of course, something unexpected happens to interfere with the smooth functioning of the machine, all the various parts of which are organized and directed by some device or other powered by . . .

" . . . by what?

" . . . by three tiny low-voltage, low-amperage batteries of some sort or another . . . centres, I think they're called . . . and . . . and . . .

" . . . but just where is this famous 'Power-Centrum' about which we hear so much just now, when I think I need it most?

"It only seems to appear at the worst possible times when I am forced by circumstances beyond my control to make efforts beyond my ordinary capacity and my attention for some reason or other happens to be on the whole of myself, I suppose, with just enough attention left over for my outer world, which seems to proceed unaccountably quickly, under the Law of Three . . .

" . . . whereas my inner world, what there is of it, seems to proceed rather like a broken wind-up toy along the lines of the Law of Seven, periodically falling into spasmodic inattention and disorientation.

"I know it ought to be the other way around, but really . . . it as as if everything inside me were made of molten lead. Nothing seems to want to move as I want it to . . .

"This very afternoon, I must begin to make a serious effort, much more serious than the efforts I made yesterday – or was it the day before? – to change all this before my machine becomes too crystallized.

"At least . . . at least . . . I have remembered to invoke my own presence into the present . . .

" . . . perhaps it just comes naturally to me. Sometimes I am amazed at my ability to fixate my attention on one idea, like self-invocation on that steel mill over there," he said, pointing to the left at a large red brick building complex, "and on those interesting cloud formations and at the same time hold an inner dialogue about the possible conversation I will have at a business appointment later this afternoon and that round sign and this car coming up fast on my left.

"He obviously wants to pass. What's the matter? Aren't I going fast enough for him?"

"It's idiots like him that give drivers a bad reputation," he continued, swinging suddenly into the left lane to catch up with the speeding car.

"Let's see, now," he began again after we had passed the other car by darting quickly around, passing him on the right, as we had feared would happen, "I should stop a moment and take stock of the situation . . .

" . . . something is definitely wrong.

"Could it be my emotional state?

"No, my emotional state is, at least for the moment, fairly

calm and quiet.

"Perhaps my sensing centrum?

"No, nothing unusual there.

"Then it must be my moving centrum on some sort of spree . . .

"No, it is not that . . .

" . . . but what could it be, if not any of these three? I know I've forgotten something, but I can't remember just what . . .

"Ah, yes, now I remember . . .

" . . . not only is all this taking place around me, but I am also part of this picture.

"My impartial presence could transform this event if only I were able to invoke myself into the present.

" . . . as it is, I am barely able to take note of what happened a fraction of a moment ago, long after the event.

"But wait! What has happened? Here it is, the middle of the afternoon, and only a moment ago . . .

" . . . it was morning and I was driving along the Hudson River and remembering to invoke myself . . .

" . . . yes, that's right . . . I was congratulating myself on my uncanny ability to remember to self-invoke and . . .

" . . . well, I *was* rather busy . . .

" . . . I had a lot of things to do . . .

" . . . first I went to the baker's, and then the bank . . . or was it the other way around?" G. concluded his hilarious monologue, to our boisterous laughter, ironic though it may have been.

CHAPTER ONE

EMOTION OF PRESENCE & MEMORY

"If we could examine with our ordinary attention the entire content of our memories as a single living, breathing wholeness, we would discover to our surprise that we really have very little detailed memory, although we were supposedly present during all those past events which form the whole of our experience in organic life," G. began, speaking to a small number of his 'drones', or kitchen helpers, during the afternoon preparation of the evening meal.

"Categorizing them with the full force of our attention," he continued, "we may be able to notice that, unlike the majority of our memories, a few memories are extremely vivid, almost as tangible and immediate as our present organic experience, and that these few unusually vivid memories from our otherwise completely forgettable past seem to include impressions of many categorical varieties from several – and perhaps all – centrums.

"For us, the important part of this is the easily observable fact that while the majority of our organic memories are either unavailable or unrecorded, or exist in very degenerated faded form, another quite different memory also exists, recorded by the same machine, yet they are extremely vivid, perhaps even as vivid as life in the present itself.

"What is vital for our work about this seemingly unimportant fact is that the very presence of these unusually vivid memories is a definite indication that some accidental momentary unobstructed connection has obviously occurred, although at present we may have no data whatever about the cause or the significance of this accidental centrum-connection.

"While these memories stand out among the vague blur of other memories not quite as vivid, a third category of memories are very vague and perhaps not exact in every detail, and others cannot be recalled at all – we only know that they must have occurred in order to account for our present existence.

"If we were able to overcome the isolation between our small organic mind and the whole attention of our non-phenomenal selves, which is commonly called the subconscious, not because it is a lesser consciousness, but because it is unavailable to the ordinary head-brain attention, and place attention on the contents of our whole memories, including the memories of cells and even of our non-phenomenal sources of attention, which have recorded all our experiences both in and out of the organic world, we might be astonished to realize just how little we are able to really remember of specific events.

"Examining those memories which are most vivid, we could make the important discovery that they always, without exception, occurred during just those moments when we were conscious by the definition of *the invocation into the present of the presence of our presence,* which is to say, the deliberate invocation of that unique source of attention existing independently of the machine's automatic mechanical attention. These momentary moments of accidental presence are characterized by the corresponding presence of *a very unique mood.*

"It is by the voluntary activation of this special mood that the corresponding state of *presence* can easily be invoked.

All higher states of consciousness have their own unique characteristic exalted moods, about which we will definitely have several talks when addressing the subject of negative emotion and exalted moods. The voluntary activation of these higher moods is the key to the voluntary invocation of various higher and lower consciousnesses," G. added, then he left the table to retire into the bedroom to rest before the evening meeting.

THE PRESENCE EXERCISE

That evening, the group sat around a large, low, square children's table, squirming uncomfortably on tiny chairs while waiting for G. to emerge from the bedroom where he rested between meals and meetings.

The adult-sized chairs, couches and tables had all been sold "for the old man's work", as he put it. The formerly quite elegant apartment was, by this evening, barren of its elaborate Victorian furnishings, needlepoint tapestries and white wool plush carpet, leaving a bare hardwood floor, some children's furnishings borrowed from a downstairs neighbor, and little else.

G. entered like a bear just out of hibernation and seemingly taking no notice of our obvious discomfort, planted his heavyset body precariously upon one of the tiny children's chairs.

We all held our collective breath, but the little chair did not collapse as we had dreaded it might, and he launched himself into the first talk of the series, *"Practical Work on Self"*.

"We tonight will make a new organization for work on self," he began, coughing slightly to clear his throat. "Without a new organization, our work may not survive another generation. I work in exile for my future family . . .

"But how to begin . . .?

"To persuade or force someone to see the necessity of

3

work is not possible, and just intellectual argument is useless. We must help him see for himself.

"One who has not seen for himself that he is not conscious and cannot make himself conscious just by deciding to, needs no argument. Theory means to him nothing at all.

"A man for whom the phenomenal veil, which rests like a funeral pall over the non-phenomenal kingdom and keeps it from profane view, has lifted, and he who has tasted even for a moment this unveiled vision and has felt himself awake for a few moments, knows instinctively that he must choose to either sleep away the remainder of his life or immediately begin efforts to awaken.

"What does this awakening mean in the real sense of the word?

"The most that any ordinary man is able to say, and then only by accident of circumstances, is 'I happen somehow to be Here Now, to my utter astonishment . . .' This form of consciousness, in which we are for a moment able to sense the presence of the real 'I' in the present, and not just the dim, automatic-imaginary 'I' of the personality, is called 'awakening'.

"In ordinary life, this seldom happens just by itself, but under the right conditions, it may sporadically occur due to certain accidental factors in ourselves and in the atmosphere.

"Four definite forms of consciousness are possible to man: Horizontal Sleep; Walking Sleep; Self-Presence; and Fixation in the unveiled Vision. *Ordinary Horizontal Sleep* and *Walking Sleep*, mechanical man can already produce in himself without our help.

"It is the third form of consciousness, *Self-Presence*, the result of fixation of certain definite forms of attention on the phenomenal veil, which he attributes to himself, but does not and cannot ordinarily possess. We must find some subtle way to introduce him to this state without too much damage to his vanity.

"*Self-Presence* is so basic' to man that he ought to be

taught as a child from infancy to live always in this state. It is like kindergarten to our efforts; if civilization lived up to its name, we would not now be forced to begin at such a low level of work.

"Man's ordinary presence resembles a worker who has fallen asleep while working, yet, just because his work continues, he does not realize he is asleep. He is unable to accept the fact that activity itself, even a complicated task, does not require his authentic presence or his voluntary fixated attention in the least.

"Ordinary man has sacrificed presence in favor of automatic machine attention, which we call 'identification', which causes him to 'fall into' everything he sees, and he will also someday die like this. In this last sense, man and his domesticated dog have at least one thing in common."

"How can we work along this line?" D. asked.

THE EXERCISE:

"To begin with, one must learn to divide attention at least a little, with half the attention on 'it', the organic self plus the outer world, and the other half on our real 'I', which can be found by tracing attention back *to the source of attention* with the use of sensing until the vision changes slightly and the phenomenal veil lifts a little . . . the ambient atmosphere will seem subjectively noticeably cooler, as during a séance, in true meditation, during a successful angelic invocation, or at a voluntary passing from this life. At the same time, the other half of attention should be firmly but gently fixated on objects of outer attention . . . say, the second-hand of a clock.

"Do this for two whole minutes without interruption in the sensing of presence of 'I'. If 'K' is not fully present or something else attracts the attention even for one moment, begin again. If prayer beads are used, count one bead for each involuntary break in attention. For the purpose of this exercise, *all* breaks in attention are involuntary.

"It is possible in six months, maybe one year, to attain the status of a 'two-minute-idiot'. An 'idiot' in this sense is anyone who struggles with his automatic phenomenal nature, his bio-psychological conditioning.

"We must not be tempted to use this higher, non-phenomenal attention in the same way as a donkey follows a carrot tied to his own head, just mentally aware of our presence . . . We must successfully, with our unified will, invoke and *sense* our presence *in the present*."

He then stood in front of the group in a bow-and-arrow pose. Indicating the forward hand holding the bow, he said, "This hand represents the world of 'it', what we can call 'the present' – the outer world, including our organic machine and its functioning centrums."

Drawing his other hand back in a smooth, swift motion, he added, "This other hand represents presence becoming, for the first time, aware of its presence in the present, by drawing away from identification with events, by observing impartially and at the same time using subjective organic sensations to *sense its own definite presence in the present.*

"This invocation of *presence in the present* eventually produces what we call *Being* in the real sense of the word . . . pure non-phenomenal electro-magnetic vibration resulting from the blending of the two primary forces represented by the passive present and the active force, *presence.*

"In ordinary life man is a phenomenal-veil-nonentity, and for him only his fixation on phenomena exists; he cannot make *Being* because *Being* is a result of the blending of two real forces. To make any vibration whatever, one must have both plus minus forces, above and below the zero-point, producing a wave with a definite frequency, amplitude and periodicity.

"When *Being* is produced, a definite and discernible sound and vibration are emitted from the organism. With my sensing apparatus – which was originally the same as yours – I am able to see and hear this vibration-of-Being.

"Only when presence is present in the present, can the First Force blend with the Second, making the Third force, *Being*."

He held one hand with fingers extended. "This will represent the phenomenal, what we call the present, the Second Force." Holding his other hand with the fingers extended in the same way, he added, "And this will represent our non-phenomenal 'presence', the First Force.

"When we blend them together," he said, at the same time meshing the fingers of both hands together, "we produce momentarily what we call *Being*. Now we can rightfully say 'I *Am* Here Now', because all three forces are at least temporarily represented.

"To attain permanent existence for our Being, we must invoke our presence many thousand times. You have the data now to decide if self-invocation will be a profitable enterprise for you before you waste too much of your precious time. Should you wish to continue, you will quickly learn that self-invocation requires a definite degree of force – not force in the ordinary sense, but as it would be understood in certain forms of martial arts, and in certain religious gatherings.

"To invoke presence with this special force, each pulsation of the body, resulting from the heartbeat, provides a natural tempo. Do not allow this effort to become automatic. Real presence must be freshly invoked for each new moment.

"All nature, along with the eager help of contemporary civilization and its power-possessors, conspire against man to make him forget his presence and to always and in everything identify with his organic self. In this way man learns eventually to be just cannon-fodder for their military, and paper-shufflers for their industrial empires.

"Man is educated to 'fall into' his outer world just as he falls into a cinema screen. He learns to forget his presence and to become whatever he sees in front of him, allowing his involuntary self to take the place of his invoked presence whenever he becomes engrossed in some reverie or activity, unless something accidentally happens to force his 'presence' to be momentarily present in the present.

"Such a man has not even the smallest presence when he dies; he has made no Being with the possibility of continuation. F. has drawn a diagram to show how this experiment should be performed."

ORDINARY MAN:

"Hereness or it"

_____

CONSCIOUS MAN:

"Here"----------------------"I"----------------------------"Now"
"Am"

"We can use this idea to help us remember to invoke our presence into the present. Repeat, but not automatically, the prayer 'I wish this to be used for the invocation of the presence of my presence into the present', whenever some 'reminding factor' such as remorse or frustration helps you to remember. Make sure you have a clear idea what 'this' refers to. It can be anything at all . . . a mood, an activity, the loss of an object, a broken glass or dish, an accident, a pain in the abdomen, the death of a friend, a special food or liqueur . . .

"Identification is not just simple attachment to the phenomenal side of the veil. It is falling into what we see before us, even into our own organic machine. To identify in this way separates our presence from the present by the isolating force of *dimension*, a common phenomenal-hallucination.

"We can learn to be like a lightning rod for the fusing of these two worlds, *making a new world* which cannot exist independently. Only in the process of voluntary evolution are we able to make this new world for the benefit of the Absolute.

"It is hard to grasp this idea, but ordinary man is so completely and continually identified with his organic machine that he cannot even separate his presence from his machine.

"The yogi takes the opposite end of this stick. He has real presence, but no presence in the present, because he rejects as illusion the phenomena around him, the Second Force. He is as a result, in general, without much Being. Third Force cannot be obtained just by pouring from the empty into the void.

"Self-consciousness is to fully *sense* presence in the present – to be present with a whole sensation of presence.

"This disarmingly simple experiment, if attempted for two full minutes without one single break in attention, however momentary, can demonstrate to anyone in his own direct experience several important facts:

1. That under ordinary conditions man is asleep . . . Not just 'man in general', but we ourselves in particular.

2. That it is possible to see, and even to taste a little, what it is to be 'not asleep'.

3. That only by special effort is it possible to really awaken.

4. The urgent necessity for work on self.

5. The exact method for waking at least a little from this sleep.

6. More or less, how much effort will be required in order to awaken even to this extent from sleep, which is to say, the automatic hypnotic fixation upon the phenomenal side of the veil?

7. Why only are we able to work on ourselves, our *Being, presence* and evolution in and for the Work, and why no one else can do this work for us?

8. That some new, hitherto unknown, source of force for our work will be required on a much larger scale than we are now accustomed to arousing in ourself.

9. That 'the Work' is very real indeed and not just philosophizing.

10. That the flow of time slips away very quickly and once lost cannot be regained; that there is a time limit for our work, and if we miss this opportunity, we may not be able to make efforts later, when we are more fixated and habitual.

"We will, in short, no longer require intellectual stimulation to convince ourselves of all this.

"One who has experienced this effort to wake up and can be honest with himself can never again, until he has mastered the invocation of presence, say without shame, '*I am here*', '*I am awake*', or '*I am conscious*'. Two minutes with the clock can show him both his fixation on phenomena and also at the same time, reveal the real possibility of becoming awake.

"To attain this third form of consciousness, even to see the necessity for it in life, is the first real test for a man who claims the right to work on himself.

"If a man really knew that he could not be present just by deciding to be present, he would be near to understanding his predicament.

"He who believes himself to be already present in the present, unified in all his parts – although as we find him in nature, man is a colony similar to the man o'war, a peculiar jellyfish composed of many different but mutually cooperative organisms – and possessing the Will of unobstructed flow of *the force*, cannot work on self. He is a slave to that involuntarily active 'some-thing' which speaks of itself in 'first person', calls itself 'I', and has a name which gives the illusion of continuity of presence, unity and will.

"The invocation of presence into the present requires continual special effort; for this we must be convinced of the necessity and feel a definite discontent with ordinary organic existence.

"Two minutes of invoked presence can be our aim for now; later, we will try to extend this to an hour or two – perhaps more.

"This is not our final goal, but at least one can see how to begin and maybe work more quickly to attain what is in the final analysis, only the ordinary state for a real three-brained man who, unlike homo sapiens, begins life free from the hallucinatory effects of the veil."

CHAPTER TWO

THE JOURNEY

The question was asked how we could embark on our own journey to accomplish a full hour or more of invoked presence into the present?

G. replied, "One hour of the unveiled vision is the result of much work over a long period of time; as you are, you could not tolerate even a few minutes of life without the veil.

"If we are able to see that not even for two minutes are we able to struggle to consciousness with full presence, we have accomplished quite enough for now. At least we know something which ordinary man does not and cannot know about himself; that he does not possess consciousness in any real sense and that with ordinary efforts, he cannot make himself conscious no matter how hard he may try.

"Tomorrow all day and for the next several days, with all your force, invoke the presence of your presence into the present, no matter in what circumstances you may happen to momentarily find yourself.

"Remember to *sense* – not just place ordinary attention on – your invoked presence. Reverberate this sensation in your solar plexus continually.

"If you should happen to once-in-a-while forget to self-invoke," he said jokingly-sarcastically, "then mentally prod yourselves with a silver fork you-know-where, and try again . . . "Soon you will be convinced you have very far to go yet, but it is not all as hopeless as it seems.

"We will not look like monkeys with all our attention becoming fixated on interior and exterior attractions, when presence is present in the present; we cannot act like boobies then, because only the machine acts unconsciously in sleep.

"To refuse to identify with the identity of the machine is to refuse ourselves the personal indulgence of 'palpitating self-oblivion', reserving such self-pampering exclusively for pleasure-seeking phenomenal aristocrats.

"We are strangers in this world and are forced to bow to its imaginary hungers until we can uninterruptedly invoke the presence of our presence into the present.

"The Law of Three is shorthand for self-invocation of presence, represented by the fixated triad, 9, 3, 6. Not even the Absolute can give us the means to make this permanent bridge between worlds; it can only be a result of continual self-initiation.

"A new candidate entering our work can first be offered this beginning experiment, to invoke his presence into the present. If as a result of this experiment he sees the necessity for work, only then he can be given more. If he is not interested, he can just continue snoring; we should not disturb his sleep.

"We must economize our effort with those new to our work, give them practical experiments which allow them to see for themselves without intellectual argument. This powerful little beginning experiment of self-invocation can help to reveal to someone already sensitive to the Work the urgent necessity for work-on-self without the necessity for external persuasion.

"With this method, the first immediate result is to see

for oneself one's utter helplessness and that at first nothing can be done about it except to use the attention, such as it is in the beginning, to observe this situation as actively as possible.

"As in gymnastics, it takes time to develop the muscles necessary for evolution. We may make efforts for years without visible change.

"In general, man travels in a form of trans space-ship from the world of phenomena to the non-phenomenal world beyond the veil, by sleep, drugs, hypnotism or accident. He does not and cannot in this way produce any permanent *Being*, the vessel in which the soul is nurtured from its first form, an immortal thing without consciousness, memory or conscience towards the Absolute. In this respect he is in exile from his possible exalted state and does not know it, because he has the psychological buffers of vanity and fear to protect his fixated vision.

"When he can learn to impartially hear, understand and respond to real ideas, only then can his life have any meaning. He must learn to respond with his presence even when surrounded by distractions. His machine can fall asleep, but never can his presence be asleep.

"When the attention is automatically fixated on outer attractions, the invocation of presence, which is a voluntary activity, is a luxury and not a necessity. This one-centered life without presence is a powerful form of world-hypnosis called *Maya*. This word *Maya* does not mean that the world itself is an illusion, but that *identification with the phenomenal side of the veil* produces the phenomenal illusion.

"We cannot feel real Being-satisfaction if we fail to use our lives for voluntary evolution. At the end, we will feel remorse if we had wasted our Life on phenomenal fixations.

"In a male, his presence is female and passive, while his organic machine is male and active. In a female, her presence is male and active, and her machine is female and passive. This is one reason that a woman cannot work in the Work – although she is able to work *for* the Work – without a male partner, except under very extraordinary conditions.

"Harmony of these two naturally opposing and unreconciling forces is impossible for ordinary man. He has no third reconciling force in himself to help them blend, and has no data how to obtain this catalytic reconciling force.

"Ordinary man is only dimly aware of these forces in himself and if he gives it any part of his attention at all, thinks of these forces in a biological sexual way, and is ashamed that his presence is the opposite of his organic sex. He is so completely identified with his organic gender that he buries his presence deeply and rejects this impossible contradiction in himself.

"Higher states of consciousness are connected with functions of higher centrums, but although they function continually even in ordinary man, their results cannot blend and are useless alchemically because his centrums are not activated and balanced.

"A correct use of attention can deepen our 'sensation of presence' and make our observation of the machine less subjective. In general, we give attention only to those flashing and glittering objects and activities which attract the monkey in us, each object of attention being categorically placed in a corresponding centrum, seldom in a sequence resembling something sane.

"Everything in organic nature is against the Work. Nature is right, and we are wrong to struggle against our ordinary destiny. We play a dangerous game when we oppose nature, the most powerful force phenomenally fixated man can know.

"We stupidly strive not to become engulfed by the phenomenal, not to allow the world and the moon to eat us alive, to swallow and digest us, then spit out what parts of us fail to serve nature's purpose.

"Nature does not fear ordinary efforts, however valiant and mighty. Time grinds every grain. We must outsmart nature, force him to make a mistake and allow us to pass from lower, phenomenal influences."

To one of the pupils, G. then said, "You are chasing a carrot tied to your own head," and added that some people are lucky – they realize they are not yet ready for work and have the opportunity to leave before they find themselves in water too deep.

"To such people, because it may be their last contact for a very long time," he explained, "if they ask for something to take with them, I offer the invocation of presence in the hope that after a while they will see for themselves that as they are, even if they knew exactly how to work, they cannot work without some catalytic force. After this little revelation, they may be ready for serious work.

"It is not always *apropos* to invoke presence. Evolved man must rest and play, but also he must sleep. To remain awake by propping the eyelids open with toothpicks even when exhausted, to serve the stupid belief that one should remain permanently conscious, is pathological. A *sensible* tempo of effort is important for good results."

CHAPTER THREE

TO BE ALIVE

"What invocation could we use for the invocation of presence?" G. asked.

"I am here," someone volunteered.

"But this is an incomplete formulation, which therefore has an opposite invocation," G. replied; "What would it be?"

"There I go?" someone humorously suggested. When the laughter died down, G. said, "Very close . . . closer than you think."

This led to an explanation of another use of the "stop". Between one exhalation and the next inhalation is a pause, a moment of temporary death, a taste of breathlessness, during which we could, if we used this moment of breathlessness as a remembering factor, practice invoking our presence in preparation for that moment when our breath really *will* come to a complete stop.

"The invocation of presence, especially under serious stress," G. continued, "is an acquired art which must be developed and improved every day and not just under easy circumstances, or it will all be just 'hark, a cannon!' until the day the cannon goes off, when we hear a hysterical scream, 'Jesus Christ, what was *that*?'

"The intentionally acquired habit of the invocation of presence does not just happen; nothing in ordinary life produces the invocation of presence, and in fact, if anything, it produces just the opposite. Nor will this invocational habit penetrate our being by osmosis just by hearing about the idea.

"Everyone here has the experience to know and understand this. Maybe you practice piano, dance or sports . . . it doesn't matter what; you know that serious mastery requires many hours of practice without missing a single day.

"What is lost in a day must be regained in a month, and to really be alive, to intentionally form the habit of the invocation of presence through the same daily routine, day after day, life after life, in that endless procession of momentary events produced by phenomenal hallucination, we must depend upon our unified will to work, which in turn depends upon our invoked presence . . .

"Do we really want it? If we really wish to take our place in the greater circle of invocation, we must be able to continually arouse the will to work, at least to use every available opportunity . . . such as this very moment . . . and when are we ever too busy to perform this invisible act of work-will, the invocation of our presence into the present?

"It requires no special activities or exterior conditions. The silent, discreet invocation of presence can be performed anywhere, under any conditions, even at a restaurant, a boiler factory, or even in prison, until it becomes second-nature."

CHAPTER FOUR

SECOND WIND PHENOMENON

G. spoke to the group one evening about the *second wind* phenomenon:

"Scientists have finally 'discovered' that there is no physiological basis for the phenomenon known as 'second wind', a fact long-known by primitive savages everywhere.

"I am sure that all of you here have experienced *something* that occurs after severe organic efforts. If there is no organic basis for this change, then we must look for a *mental basis* for this 'second wind' phenomenon. Mentate on what this could be.

"The 'second wind' phenomenon is an artificial *mental* barrier which can be broken by prolonged efforts of the moving centrum. 'Second wind' occurs with other things – work ideas not the least. Prolonged Movements and rhythmics can produce this 'second wind'.

"The so-called 'psychic' is a person who, for one reason or another, usually as a result of extreme anxiety, has automatically achieved the psycho-emotional 'second wind' in which psychic-force-data becomes accessible. There is also a non-phenomenal 'second wind' and a sexual 'second wind', both of which are only activated when all automatic biological drives have been exhausted.

"To achieve any 'second wind,' we must 'go the whole hog including the postage,' which is to say, to walk the extra mile.

"Transformation is the 'second wind' of being," he told the group that afternoon. "There is no organic barrier, just psychological. We must achieve the second wind of presence, after we can do all our exercises effortlessly, naturally and easily every day, all day long."

"It seems we may sometimes achieve this second wind of presence for short moments of time," said P. "but how do we keep it going?"

Replied G., "We must make intentional use of real emotion.

"We will fail continually until the day we wake up in terror because we suddenly realize that we really *do* fall asleep on our feet.

"Then, suddenly, the exercises become important to us, and after a while, they form themselves as a function of our natural existence.

"If we do not realize that we fall asleep standing up, and care nothing for the result of this in our lives, then these exercises will seem impossible; not even for one second can we invoke presence.

"One test of whether a man is awake or not is if he is forced by the terror of the situation to struggle for the invocation of his presence. If he does not feel particularly inclined to struggle for his real life, and is content with ordinary organic survival, we know at least one thing about him and his chances for work."

"Is the second wind of presence achieved through a series of efforts and failures at invocation?" J. asked.

"The invocation of presence will not just happen by itself in the ordinary course of life," he replied, "but on the other hand, invoking mechanically, no matter how fanatically, does not guarantee results either.

"What is needed is a catalyst, which always appears in its most ordinary form as a mirror of our own phenomenal hallucinations . . .

"The catalyst is also sometimes called the Holy Ghost. The Holy Ghost has consciousness, whereas Grace – divine as it is – is unconscious, automatic and, in this sense at least, although without it, real evolution is impossible, completely useless.

"Because this may take years, we must also embark upon many other lines of work, and all lines of work must begin at once without delay.

"Our work-time is quickly running out. We wake up one morning and our lives are over . . . finished. It is too late then for feelings of remorse to have any effect, except to serve as the source of force for one final *invocation of presence.*

"Awakening is not the end of work on self, it is the very beginning of work on self. *A man who is not awake cannot work on himself, only on his awakening.*

"What if we found ourselves at the end of life, bound to eternal existence on a deserted island, with no hope of rescue now or at any time in the future?

"If we could only bring one thing with us from this island of organic life to the deserted island to which we will be brought when we pass from this world, what would we bring?

"This is not an imaginary exercise; someday soon we will be brought to just such an island, and we must be prepared to exist there without those personal amusements upon which we have learned to depend for our artificial civilized sanity.

"To live among the dead, we must also be dead; at least we must die to the ordinary preoccupations of the phenomenal side of the veil.

"When our presence blends with the non-phenomenal, the path divides itself in dark and light," G. said, holding his two index fingers together, pointing up and then separating them slightly in an angle to form a V.

"Those who use the dark side of this force, abuse without shame these petty little mental and emotional powers to take from organic life whatever they can to feed their sensual hungers, and to control events, immersing themselves still deeper in the momentum of organic life. Hopefully, after you have mastered this exercise, you will still have the courtesy and the sense to pay the bus fare.

"To blend perfectly with the flow of force, we must be annihilated, and if, after annihilation, we can continue to function in a work-way, which is to say, to continue to serve in the circle of invocation regardless of our organic hungers, then perhaps we can learn to work for the benefit of the non-phenomenal side of the veil.

"If organic hungers within us are still alive, the invocation of presence is interrupted, and we are not dead, not annihilated – we have not died before our ordinary organic death."

In response to a question from one of the French members of the group, he said, "Sometimes when first practicing the diffusion of vision, portions of the phenomenal world may disappear. *When in doubt, go limp;* soon your vision will adjust.

"The second wind of vision, the unveiled vision, is as a man ought to see; not imaginary phenomenal effects, but in the spectrum of the non-phenomenal kingdom, which is ordinarily obscured by the veil."

G. commented to a member of the group, who was doing some needlepoint during the meeting, that this was an appropriate task to be working at during such assemblies and that among special work-communities, this was very commonplace.

He added that handcrafts such as knitting, crocheting, sewing, weaving and prolonged sex are useful moving centrum tasks to combine with meetings.

We didn't know how literally to take this last,

admittedly very appealing, advice, so the majority of us remained dressed and continued as before.

"Real knowledge only comes in special states, and can be transmitted and understood only in special states," he explained. "Handcrafts set the stage for second wind if efforts are made to achieve extreme attention to detail.

"Just before the second wind of personal annihilation is achieved, a sense of imminent failure will descend upon you like a vulture on an inattentive mouse.

"This artificial emotional barrier, the sensation of apprehension, is a safety factor. Before we achieve anything serious, we may decide to stop for our own safety, realizing that the body could collapse and die, or worse. And so certain invocational methods are introduced only at advanced stages in the preparatory work, initiated by voluntary initiation and, fortunately for the continued momentum of the organic machine, the second wind of personal annihilation is not easily achieved.

"This process of voluntary self-annihilation is known as the Ten Thousand Deaths, because each time personal annihilation is almost near, we draw back, and the veil invariably falls – except for the last time – and we must begin again.

"No objective barrier exists to prevent success, only a subjective barrier to the second wind of personal annihilation, about which we will talk again sometime very soon.

"The second wind of presence is called the Non-phenomenal Vision, and this vision indicates that the *invocation of presence* has been attained, at least momentarily.

"We must be able to easily recognize this state if we are to know whether our efforts at self-invocation and its accompanying sensation of an emotional cleansing as our presence washes over the phenomenal self, are effective. How can we expect to succeed in our work within the circle of invocation, in which we invoke the really large presences – which require subtlety and finesse far beyond what is required

for the invocation of our own comparatively puny presences –
if we have no sensing experience to indicate when we
successfully invoke ourselves?

"At first we may have only a momentary non-
phenomenal vision to indicate to ourselves the successful
invocation of the presence of our presence into the present. In
the Eastern tradition this was called *Satori*.

"This vision, even though only momentary, is
sufficient to indicate a successful invocation of presence,
because only during the invocation of presence can the
unveiled vision reveal itself.

"When we first begin to seriously use non-phenomenal
vision as a definite indication of the successful invocation of
presence, we notice that, although the vision came easily to us
the very first time, it was difficult – perhaps even impossible –
to attain again a second or a third or even a fourth time, and
the harder we try, the farther we seem to fall from this exalted
state of grace until it seems impossible that we will ever
achieve it again . . .

"This phenomenon is common in any newly acquired
skill, and is particularly noticeable in a new sexual encounter.
A common reaction is to leave and then return, hoping that the
first easy success will come again.

"And often it does, in the same way that a lover might
be more exciting after a prolonged absence . . .

"But if we really understand how to work, we will not
depend upon this artificial success, even though we may lose
sight of the vision in our early efforts.

"If we know anything about real efforts, we will
remember that with serious effort, our penetration of the veils
will far surpass that of the lover who comes and goes
periodically, enamored of 'instant benefits'.

"After several months or even years of practice, the
vision may return in varying periods of several minutes at a
time. This, in the Eastern tradition, was called *dhyana*.

"Perhaps years later, the original state will be re-achieved and surpassed far beyond the first easy glimpse.

"When the non-phenomenal vision becomes continuous with the continuous invocation of presence, the possibility exists, for the very first time, of becoming a serious candidate for the Work.

"In the Eastern tradition, this continuous state of presence and its corresponding non-phenomenal vision were called *samadhi*, meaning the undifferentiated unveiled vision of the world.

"This unveiled vision, in which everything blends into a flat patchwork quilt of light and dark, color and form, without individual significance, and particularly without the dimension of depth, separation of forms and objects and the illusion of perspective, is usually misunderstood as an 'out of body experience', but is really just the unveiled vision of Creation.

"Eventually, although it may take a very long time before one attains permanent presence and the corresponding unveiled vision, one is able to adjust to this vision while still performing activities of the machine, taking responsibility for them – recognizing the objective unreality and, at the same time, the subjective reality of the phenomenal vision and its invocational apparatus appearing as ordinary objects, treating everything encountered with respect and care, as if they represented something in the unveiled vision, as in fact they do.

"Even though individuals, within the phenomenal vision, are simply shadows passing over the Face, they represent the presence and the present mood of our endless creator. When one is awake, one can respond to this, knowing exactly how this vision represents the mood in the moment.

"In the unveiled vision, colors become brighter or all color vanishes and objects may have their own internal luminescence.

"Vision becomes sharper, clearer, but individual objects will seem at the same time somehow more indistinct, more distant, more a part of a larger living whole than an isolated solid object.

"Sensation will intensify and everything will seem clearly connected to everything else and to oneself.

"Objects and events will take on a new meaning . . . perhaps many different new meanings.

"None of these effects will seem at the time contradictory, although later they may not make rational sense.

"A faint sound of choral music or high-pitched buzzing may occur, alternated with periods of muffled, deadened silence.

"Movement of any kind may tend to be sluggish, similar to the slowed-down actions of a mime. The atmosphere may seem fragrant and honey-like. Along with this may come a feeling of euphoria or elation.

"Everything seems delicate and exquisite; a feeling of warmth and friendliness seems to emanate from all objects, which seem suddenly alive, possessing their own definite consciousness. The attention of the surroundings upon you becomes very obvious.

"There may be an occasional urge to giggle or laugh aloud at the irony of it all, and at the same time, a feeling that the stillness and hushed atmosphere ought to be maintained, as in a church.

"There is a profound feeling that you know something very great but inexpressible, and at the same time, an exalted indifference to it all.

"These are some of the signs of the unveiled vision. There are other indications that presence has been successfully invoked. Some of these indications may lead directly to temporary or permanent placement in a home reserved for very special people just like yourself, and so it is strongly suggested that you resist the temptation to wear, on the lapel, some button which tells any interested – and also at the same time, an equal number of disinterested – party or parties that you have occasionally achieved the unveiled vision."

CHAPTER FIVE

PRESENCE: A SERIOUS CONFESSION

G. asked, "How is it that the machine is able to surprise us with unexpected actions: That we somehow, more than just occasionally, find ourselves doing things we never intended to do?"

Several students started to answer and G. motioned them to be still. "This is not a question to be answered immediately, simply to pour words out of your empty mouths into the equally empty void of your restless, wandering attention," he cautioned. About twenty minutes later he continued his talk.

"The 'I' which has been surprised . . . *where has it been all this time?* Why does the non-phenomenal presence fail to exert continuous authority over the machine?

"Why is the machine able to initiate foul deeds, far from our highest intentions and strongest vows, appalling and even devastating in their totality of personal and impersonal effects, without our knowledge or consent?

"And why is it that, even when we are aware of 'crimes of the machine' against our work destinies, we are seemingly unable to exercise even the smallest authority to make the machine obey our supposedly conscious intentions?

"A question could be used as an exercise by the group: 'In what ways exactly have your machines surprised you against your higher intentions?'

"If this question is to be used for real work, you must answer completely honestly, not considering possible personal embarrassment, or the damage to your precious feelings of security, vanity or imaginary self-esteem.

"It is a real confession in every sense of the word and a real candidate for work must someday answer for the honesty and authenticity of this answer given to the group today.

"We can lose any serious hope of candidacy for the work by a failure to answer this call for solemn confession.

"Lies, omissions or refusal to answer are serious self-crimes, as serious for the candidate as if I refused to answer a question asked with necessity.

"We must never be too busy, too lazy or unwilling to answer a real question. If we answer all serious questions with serious answers, we are given the grace to ask questions of our own and can, because we do not hide personal secrets locked away in a citadel of anticipation of exposure and possible humiliation, expect to receive real answers to our questions."

The group, under his direct supervision, proceeded to assemble possible categories in which answers to this question might fall:

1. The *"Oh, No, Not Again"* syndrome in general, as in "What? Don't tell me I'm doing *this* again?" For example, just finding oneself in bed with someone one did not intend to have sex with, which G. had been heard to call the "falling between the sheets" category.
2. Oral sphincter addictions
    A. Delicious foods
    B. Alcohol, cigarettes and drugs
3. Impulse buying

4. Negative manifestations
5. Procrastination in general
6. "Booby manifestations" – finding yourself with your finger up your nostril after having sworn to yourself you would never pick your nose in public ever again.

Earlier, G. had given us a useful clue to self-invocation, mentioning that if something periodically self-arising in the machine were truly habitual, we must not say we would do it again, that a habit would only entrench itself more firmly if we tried to disallow it, but that it could serve as a powerful sensing-centrum remembering factor to help us remember – as our attention wanders aimlessly through daydreams, fantasies and periods of involuntary self-oblivion – to invoke the presence of our presence into the present.

In this sense, as a remembering device which works because it contains *definite noticeable sensations* – usually sensations of some form of remorse – our habits and even our complete lack of authority over the organic machine, become invocational tools for the evolution of our being.

G. also suggested we ask ourselves *why* we make vows we know we cannot keep, and which we secretly know we never really intend to keep.

CHAPTER SIX

THREE LEVELS OF WORK

"Presence is the only *discernible* 'something' which is non-phenomenal. If we mistakenly say 'I' when we really refer to the machine, we must find a way to bring this involuntary lie to our instant attention.

"But how do we know which 'I' is which? We must learn to really stop, look and listen . . .

"For example, the organic machine may desire a glass of Armagnac, but 'I' care nothing for the things of this world, particularly food and drink. It leaves these hungers to those animal forms and lower organic consciousnesses who wander the world in search of pleasures, amusement and superficial organic satisfactions.

"If, when referring to the machine, we happen to somehow involuntarily lose the attention and substitute 'I' when we really mean the machine's 'I', we should find an appropriate reminding factor.

"In this series of exercises, one must, in this case, always refer to the machine in the third person 'it' . . . as in, 'it wishes a glass of Armagnac'.

"When referring to parts of the machine, we must

remember to refer to the part and not to the whole of the machine, and definitely not in the possessive, which is to say, '*the* hand itches' not '*my* hand itches', or 'I' itch . . .

"Unconscious forms of possessive identification suggested by the ordinary language of organic sleep can, if we know how to use the sensation of remorse, become for us a tool of self-remembering.

"This new view of the presence exercise will be the first penetration beyond the surface. It is the first serious exercise."

Someone asked, "Is there also an esoteric form of these exercises?"

G. replied, "If not, then we are wasting each other's time. For the preparatory sensing, feeling, and mentating series of exercises, there is a beginning-obligatory form, a mesoteric form and a special hidden form.

"The exact method is given in the first form; its rough centrum of gravity indicated in the second form; and in the third form, the mantle is lifted and the corresponding view of the unveiled kingdom is revealed directly, through a transforming initiation."

"Then the exercises you gave at the beginning are not objective?" someone asked from the back of the room.

"They are objective only in their esoteric form," G. explained, "but the esoteric is given only when one has earned a 'diploma of authentic understanding' in the mesoteric. This, in turn, depends upon not just mental familiarity, a passing acquaintance engendered by the head brain which can be expressed in the following way: '*Aha! I can see the results of this exercise, so since I can see its purpose and I have already performed the exercise eleven times, no sense going on any further . . . let us just say that imaginary success is the same as genuine success and be done with it!*'

"This is the usual course of a false man's struggle with himself and clearly shows to us how exactly the secret keeps itself.

34

"Real initiation requires serious concentrated effort and the attention of the sensing centrum to insure that our efforts are not merely imaginary.

"Never will we be able to 'just think ourselves out of this mess'.

"Before the inevitable personal annihilation provided by dear nature occurs involuntarily to our organic machines, propelling us head-over-heels through the veil, we must discover the means to use our activities productively *for our Being* and for the greater good.

"Before our annihilation destroys our chance to work for the non-phenomenal side of the veil, we must evolve into a definite unique place in the Work."

"It seems to me," said J., "that exoteric ideas are given freely, mesoteric ideas are just hinted at and esoteric ideas are a definite 'second wind phenomenon' produced by special effort in the first two forms. This seems to me to be the process of initiatism as you have described it. I wish to know if my formulation is correct and complete, or is there more to it that I cannot yet see?"

"I could provide you with three answers, all different, each suggesting new questions and experiments," G. replied. "In the first place, your formulation is correct and complete; in the second place, you *could* dig deeper; and in the third place . . . Ach, but why even talk about the third place?" G. laughed deeply, lapsing into complete silence which continued through the remainder of the evening.

At dawn, G. went off to the market with a few helpers to shop for the next evening's food.

CHAPTER SEVEN

ON INVOKING PRESENCE

"The phenomenal world can – and should – be viewed as a giant theater in which every phenomenal form is a character within which every participating non-phenomenal presence has a definite part to play.

"It can easily be seen how everyone can play his or her part either voluntarily or involuntarily, either well or badly, but if we are players on a stage, for whose benefit is this eternal, perpetual performance, in which each moment is captured and frozen forever in a matrix of space and time, through which our non-phenomenal attention passes as a wandering traveler, producing the compelling illusion of personal participation and even self-initiated action?

"Involuntary life can be transformed by effectively invoking the presence of one's presence into the present and then voluntarily playing one's corresponding voluntary part in the phenomenal world, at which time, it suddenly becomes possible to study and to learn our corresponding non-phenomenal roles in the Unveiled Kingdom by the observation of the resulting unveiled vision . . ."

Asked if he would be willing to demonstrate this unveiled vision, he answered with a sigh, "Once maybe when I was young, I might do for a pretty young lady . . . now, I can only afford to perform these little tricks for a very rich dowager with a correspondingly fat checkbook – of course *strictly* for the benefit of the Work . . . !" He threw his head back and rumbled with deep laughter at his own joke which was, by and large, lost upon most of the group.

"Under certain special conditions," he continued, "it is possible to temporarily or momentarily, artificially lift the phenomenal veil, taking the opportunity to see how easy it would be if our vision were unobstructed by organic conditioning, to attach to the various impressions and sensations proceeding at any particular moment, any significance whatever.

"For the moment, at least, while temporarily free from the influence of the phenomenal veil, one is also momentarily free from the influences of organic fixations, and is able to accept new categories of visions and ideas, new lamps for old, although the organic fixations will soon reassert themselves.

"When the non-phenomenal presence is isolated from the organic present, one may feel the higher emotion of 'irony', detached from the sensations of sarcasm or cynicism; one may observe the activities of the machine-world in utter isolation from significance; in the middle of it all, one may feel the impulse to laugh at the inexorable momentum of the organic machinery of 'life', that almost infinite colony of endless repetitions of one thing appearing in a variety of changing forms, flowing over the face of the patchwork quilt, the white robe of many colors, the vision straying first to one fraction of the One, and then to another . . ." he said, lapsing into silence for some time.

After several minutes, R. asked a question she had been reserving for what seemed like the right time . . .

"I have been making attempts to place my source of attention in various locations in my body, to see where it reverberates naturally," she said.

"Where did you get such an idea?" G. thundered. "You have not now enough to do without inventing new ideas? Think of yourself as a factory worker in an assembly line, working quietly without fantasy or glamour.

"I do not wish to discourage the spirit of experimental adventure and, especially since your idea is a useful one, something which has a definite place in your work to prepare yourself to take your place in the Great Circle of Invocation. But first a factory worker must learn to live with boredom and repetition," he added, in a softer tone.

"We all begin our careers as factory workers only when we agree to descend intentionally to the lowest gallery in the factory, as ordinary production-line workers. This first struggle against our vanity, our belief in some imaginary exalted state which is our supposed birthright, really the first barrier to work, precedes all other work, even the earliest attempts to obtain data about the work . . .

"The highest idiot in the work-sense is the ordinary idiot, but there are two definite kinds of ordinary idiots, the organic-momentum variety, to which all human beings automatically belong without effort of any kind on their parts, and the ordinary idiot of the factory worker variety, who has intentionally descended from the exalted state of imaginary grace enjoyed by all human beings everywhere, and who never assumes the title of 'expert' on any subject.

"You must decide someday, and perhaps sooner than you think, which kind of idiot you are now, and which you wish to become."

CHAPTER EIGHT

MOMENTUM OF INVOCATION

THE UNIVERSAL TRAVELLING JUNK SHOP

G. remarked that the Fourth Way is also called the Way of the Fool, who uses his organic machine's mechanical weaknesses and hungers to his own advantage, for his evolution and to help him in his self-invocations and other preparatory work.

"This calls to mind the subject of the remembering factor," he continued, "which can be anything that serves to remind us to invoke presence.

"The invocation of presence depends entirely on the ability to *remember* to invoke presence.

"In the same way, the popcorn exercise and its resulting reversal of the function of the head-brain and tail-brain depends on your ability to remember to do the exercise."

"But is this not similar to the experience of not riding a bicycle for many years and then when you climb on a bicycle, the ability to ride just comes back to you as you begin peddling it all over town?" one of the younger American women asked.

G. said, "If you practice dance or theatrical arts, how do you remember to practice? A natural dancer, when practicing, engages what we call the mental-reflexive and notates movements by sensing.

"But dance is dance. A dancer cannot fail to remember to take class; in dance there are many forceful reminders.

"But self-invocation is different. Nobody pays us to self-invoke, nor does self-invocation elicit applause . . .

"So . . . How to remember to invoke presence?

"We could put up a sign . . . we will see the writing on the wall and remember to do it. But if the sign is always up, eventually it blends with the totality of visual vibrations and becomes just another dull blob of gray in the vague clutter of half-and-quarter-perceived visions, which form the greater part of the life of man on *earth* . . .

"To be really certain to remember to invoke presence, every few minutes an entirely different alarm clock would be necessary, because the same remembering factor would soon become familiar and trite . . . *Ho hum, I invoke presence, I invoke presence, invoke presence, presence, presence . . .*" he droned in a dull, flat tone.

"The invocation itself would become automatic and formal and ritualized. Ritual simply means to follow format. But ritualized in this sense means that the format has become more important than the content. If an activity becomes ritualized, the actual conditions are not taken into account – leaving no room for improvisation."

"There is the problem," R. said. "You improvise and make the scene work, come alive, but so often we do not."

G. said, "As in a play, if you plow through, the sheer luck of your straight line effort may occasionally produce the invocational effect. But as in a play, the inability to improvise generally guarantees that seldom, if ever, will it become infused with the living force of presence.

"We need a remembering factor to remind us to make each scene of the play of life come alive in the spotlight of presence.

"Suppose we saw an automobile driving on the street by itself. Could this act as a reminder for us? Anything of an unusual nature could serve to help us to remember. And after you develop a certain discipline for the invocation of presence, you will notice many remembering factors all around you in the course of ordinary life.

"You may work very hard to invoke presence four times each hour, like clockwork . . . if grudgingly, dutifully, the invocation of presence is ritualized. What could serve as a remembering factor?" he asked.

"I use thoughts as remembering factors," R. said.

"What about when thoughts become trite?" G. asked.

"In Sufi literature, there is reference made to something called *remembering*, but not what *remembering* refers to, because *remembering* in our tradition refers to different things at different stages, placing attention differently at each gradation along the way.

"For your work just now, *remembering* refers to the invocation of presence.

"Remembering to invoke presence and then *actually taking a moment to invisibly invoke presence* is the beginning of work-discipline.

"At a certain point, remembering refers to the unveiled vision of the Patchwork Quilt, 'the living Face of our endless – in the sense of the endless knot, or the endlessness of that without borders, separations or boundaries – creator.'

"Remembering can also refer to any sensation which produces negative emotion, which in turn should, by its automatic force, arouse your sleeping or wandering attention, which reminds you to invoke presence; the invocation of presence reminds you to do the popcorn exercise; the popcorn exercise reminds you to clarify the unveiled vision, which in turn reminds you to walk between raindrops; which in turn reminds you to do the last hour of life exercise; which in turn reminds you to remember to observe your pulse, which reminds you do the pulse-prayer . . .

"Then suddenly you have the definition of negative emotion which reminds you . . . *'Oh, I am supposed to remember something . . . something that starts with a P . . . provokes . . .? I could probably rationally mentate on it. Let us see if something suggests itself A,B,C . . . D, I think it starts with . . . my . . . last hour of death?'*

" 'Oops,' I feel remorse . . . What? . . . remorse? Remorse . . . I feel so guilty when I feel remorse, because I know I should feel more remorse than I do.

" 'Remorse should remind me of something, but what?

" 'No matter what I think I see, the King is naked . . .

" 'All phenomena is illusion . . .

" 'There is something I am supposed to remember . . . something . . . something . . . something . . . something . . . something . . .

" 'My habits carry me through.

" 'Even if I cannot remember the four lines, I did remember that there are four of them, just like the ten commandments. I may not know what any of them are exactly, but I do remember that there are ten of them . . .'

"Steering the sequence of associations back to the more obvious work ideas," G. continued, "because we have an associative brain, anything could remind us to work . . . This idea, using our ordinary habits and weaknesses for our work, and especially for self-invocation, is the fulcrum by which we gain evolutionary authority over the machine and suck our own blood, which is to say, drawing alchemical substances from the ordinary chemical factory of the organic functions, for the benefit of the Work and for our work-life.

"Just as M. may swear off movies, yet go to the cinema."

"Is this because I am attracted to how I behave at the theater?" M. asked.

"No, it is an addiction," G. replied. "M., you will simply *find* yourself in a theater. You may have no intention of going to the cinema and even outline other plans, but you will end up in a theater and find yourself watching a film. In the same way, someone who has decided to quit smoking will, several hours later, suddenly to his astonishment and horror, find himself smoking a cigarette.

"If you do not know your Chief Weakness, you do not have a handle on your machine and have not done your homework, which is to say, self-study, the careful and attentive observation of the machine to discover useful weaknesses which can provide the automatic force of attention for your work . . ."

"I've noticed a sarcastic reaction toward people I don't like," R. admitted. "Then at the certain crucial point, I verbalize sarcastically my observation. This happens often, because people evoke it out of me."

"You do not wish to necessarily stop," G. said.

"I could not stop if I wished to," R. replied.

"I work at my daily tasks out of guilt because people will otherwise think badly of me," D. confessed.

"Smoking is my weakness," T. said.

"Examine yourself as if you are confessing," G. said, "but these little confessions are nothing, So . . . continue your confession."

"My Chief Weakness is being an involuntary slave, performing automatically whatever I am asked to do at the moment, not examining the request," K. said, "I am a slave to approval from others."

"I am known to procrastinate on occasion," L. said, provoking some laughter.

"I am stubborn," K.W. admitted.

"My Chief Weakness is my tendency to try to draw attention to myself and to evoke laughter from people by being a clown," R. said. "And then another tendency I have is being attached to people or activities sometimes."

"Oral gratification would be one of my Chief Weaknesses," C. said. "Another weakness would be that I realize I am working very hard, but at what?"

"What you are referring to is a form of oblivion," G. said, "a taste of death. It is just like being dead, being totally identified with something."

"Making people feel guilty is my Chief Weakness," W. said.

"My Chief Weakness would be oral gratification as well as sneakiness," P. admitted.

"These confessions will change as your vision of the machine clarifies and you can discover more objectively what your Chief Weakness is," G. said.

"Suggestibility is a Chief Weakness of organic man. It can be used to provoke a series of exercises – one thing suggests another. You cannot eliminate this tendency by ordinary means, nor should you wish to, because you can use your tendency of suggestibility, the associative function, for the exercise of self-invocation . . .

"Just as the presence exercise – 'I invoke my presence into the present' – is more effective because the invocation of presence is a magical act, when you say, 'I am here now,' you can understand what you have said, agree to it, realize it, and arrive at its truth as in a deduction process.

"The invocation of presence may, for a long time, be imaginary, but some day you may hear thunder; you will discover that you have actually invoked your presence into the present and will ask yourself, 'What do I do now?' And then you must continue in a determined, if slightly trembling inner voice, 'I hereby invoke my presence into the present . . .'

"Actors perform for nearly their entire career and then one day they walk onstage and stage fright overcomes them," M. said. "They forget their lines or turn away from the audience or even freeze."

"Stage fright has plagued even some of the best, most well-known actors," G. continued, "who succumbed to it at one time or another, even at the height of their careers. Of what are they afraid?"

"Perhaps their effect on the audience," M. offered. "Most actors seem rather vain and self-important."

"From my experience," P., who had been a professional actress, said, "sometimes it suddenly comes to me that I find myself doing something onstage without really knowing how I came to be there . . . I catch myself in the middle of a line which came so automatically that I scarcely knew how I got there, or exactly where I am.

"In those moments when I wonder who I am . . . am I the character or an actress playing a character? . . . I can feel what stage fright, if it were allowed to blossom full-blown, would feel like, and even the mild attacks I have experienced now and again make it almost impossible to go on. I feel lost, alone, disoriented, but that doesn't really say it."

"Do you mean to tell us," chuckled G., "that stage fright is the result of a mild, accidental invocation of *presence?*"

"Yes, that is exactly what it must be," she agreed.

"Then we must be prepared if presence catches us in an accidental spotlight on the stage of life!" he exclaimed. "Ordinary actors and actresses may not understand what has happened to them, but for *you,* there is no excuse!

"You are aware of the invocation of presence, and by now should have observed that on occasion this can sometimes occur accidentally in the course of ordinary events.

"If none of the exercises given in this special academy of ours are of any use, then just review *all* your remembering factors. Nothing is without *some* use.

"In addition to the exercises, your group also has such songs as 'Turkish Coffee' . . ." He asked the group to sing this song, with guitar accompaniment provided by a folksinger member of the group, Parker Dixon, who had written many of the songs based on talks at G.'s table . . .

Brew me a cup of Turkish coffee,
Brew it as careful as you can.
I don't care if it takes forever,
'Cause I'm an impartial man.

First time he brewed it for the Father,
Second time he brewed it for the Son,
Third time he brewed it for the Holy Ghost.
Then it was finally done.

"I don't know what to do with impartiality," P. commented as the song concluded, "it just reminds me to invoke presence, or to try to . . . it seems that sometimes even the invocation of presence can become automatic," she added.

"Yes, that seems to be true for me, too," M. said, and several members of the group nodded in agreement.

"How do we remedy mechanicality in our invocations of presence?" P. asked, although the question was obviously in the air as several others started to ask the same thing.

"For mechanicality, the cure comes with time," G. replied. "Really, there are no hard rules, nor can there be, because if we allow ourselves to fall into firm rules for invocation, it is certain to become not just mechanical, but completely ritualized, just a formality, as the Buddhists now greet each other by bowing, supposedly in recognition of one another's non-phenomenal self, but really it has become little more than a businessman's limp dead-fish handshake and wide, enthusiastic, but totally vacant, smile.

"These little songs can be the catalyst which catches you in the spotlight of your attention, helping you to discover yourself onstage, perhaps in the middle of delivering some line or other . . .

G. paused and lifted his arms, beginning a complicated series of rhythmics. "If one thing does not bring you out of your wandering daydreams," he continued, "then something else may . . .

48

"Everything can be a remembering factor for the invocation of presence," he said, increasing the speed of the rhythmic exercise slightly, "even other exercises can serve as remembering factors, whether successful or not – even *forgetting* to perform the exercise can serve as a remembering factor, because we can use the organic sensation of remorse both as a remembering factor *and* as a source of force for our invocation.

"Why, that son of a bitch," he suddenly exclaimed, "he told me I was the only one . . . *I believed it, I believed it was true, but . . . where are you?"* he sang in a boomy, deep voice. It was one of the folk songs the group had written together.

"Where are you?" he asked again. *"Now this gives me an idea. After all, doesn't the ordinary mental attention of the head-brain function entirely by association?*

"In which case, as long as it functions by association anyway, why not use this unfortunate situation to my own advantage?

"Yes, why not allow the associations to cause me to remember to invoke my presence into the present . . . something like jiu-jitsu, in which we use an opponent's own weight and force to defeat him?

"Where are you?" he repeated. *"This reminds me of something . . . but what? To whom does the 'you' in the song refer?*

"It could be anyone, but it happens also to remind me that I am not really here at this moment, and yet I could easily be present . . .

"Yes, presence is not all that difficult, it just requires a little something from me, something that wouldn't really interfere with any of my other activities, and no one else will ever be the wiser, so it won't embarrass me or my companions . . . After all, it only takes a moment of my time to silently invoke my presence . . .

"And so I will, I will invoke my presence . . . I hereby invoke the presence of my presence into the present," he said,

sitting back just a little.

"Now we will wait for results," he continued: *"I can tell by certain definite alterations in vision, emotion and sensation . . . by which I mean that I feel clean, my state is washed away, drained by some sort of cleansing radiation which comes over me as my presence descends into the present and settles into the organic body . . . that my invocation has succeeded.*

"And I am not the only one who should be able to tell that my presence has descended into the present," he continued, *"others should also feel this cleansing effect as my vibrations of presence reverberate outward to a distance of about ten feet . . .*

"But now I have lost it; invocation is only momentary in any case, and very soon the organic self-reasserts itself, resuming its unending emission of bad vibrations, turning everything and everyone within its sphere of influence into one or another form of fertilizer.

"But as it happens, I find myself sitting here with a group of people at a large table, surrounded by other tables.

"If I were to count the people here, I would say that there are at least seventy, and yet, the chamber is very small, intended for a single family of perhaps six members . . .

"It somehow reminds me of a Hollywood version of the Last Supper, which happens to also remind me of the Last Hour of Life, another exercise which I forgot to do today . . .

"But this sensation of remorse, as I look back at all the time I have wasted in my life when I could have been working . . .

"This sensation and the corresponding thoughts which are aroused at the same time provide me with something . . . but what?

"Now I remember . . . They provide me with the force necessary for the invocation of my presence, but unfortunately I haven't really got the time just now for all that, because I'm eating . . .

50

"But I have almost finished my dinner and I realize that during the whole course of the meal, I have completely forgotten to try to transubstantiate my food as I chew and swallow it.

"How many bites did I take? What did I eat for dinner just now? I cannot even recall having eaten and, except for my empty plate and used napkin, I have no real evidence that dinner was served to me personally.

"What a waste . . . Here I am in the midst of a work-community, and I cannot even remember to eat my food in a work way!

"Imagine that! Surrounded by others, all of whom no doubt did not fail to transubstantiate their food, and I cannot remember to do the same!

"But this reminds me of something else . . . Surrounded by creatures who wish to eat my higher blood . . .

"Yes, lunar parasites, all around me, and because I forgot to invoke my presence, which is a banishing for them and which prevents them from eating my higher substances, they have had quite a feast tonight at my expense!

"But it wasn't just tonight. All during the day I was with other people, and if I didn't do something to produce organic emotions in them for the benefit of their lunar parasites, they aroused them in me for the benefit of mine.

"Yes, it's easy to see how the folk sayings came about . . . I scratch your back and you scratch mine . . . one hand washes another . . . Now I can see that these really refer to the process of reciprocal feeding, all for the benefit of lunar parasites . . .

"I may have fed them all day long, but not now, not at this very moment, because I have a weapon . . . the invocation of presence.

"It somehow reminds me of the Lone Ranger or the cavalry, riding to the rescue, but never mind, I will try it . . . perhaps it will afford me a moment or two of relief from the greedy vampires . . .

"My lunar parasites don't want me to just sit here and invoke my presence. They are hungry. They want me to get myself involved in an argument.

"Maybe I will forget all about this lunar parasite business and just read a Valentine's card; it makes me so happy . . . Sneezy . . . Grumpy . . . Doc . . .

"Now I remember . . . several years ago, the members of a work group took those names to help them remember their chief weaknesses so they could guard against the loss of angelic substances.

"But what good are they?

"How can something you can't see be of any use? What good is it to produce food for angelic invocation, anyway?

"And what are the others sitting here with me doing? Are they also having these same thoughts? I wish this to be used for the benefit of all beings everywhere, but what exactly is the 'this' to which that prayer refers?

"I cannot think of anything to do with this just now; it doesn't seem possible to make a prayer from these stupid thoughts . . .

"I'll just relax for a while, maybe drift off to sleep for a few moments . . .

"Ah, yes, the sleep exercise. I observe my machine as it arranges itself in a pseudo-sleeping, semi-horizontal posture in mimicry of sleep.

*"What was that noise in the kitchen just now? No, not a noise, a sound. All sounds are from a single source, which recalls to mind the famous Muses and the composer Beethoven, who told his wife that she was his inspiration, to which she answered in the tones of his fifth symphony, not yet written, 'What, me? Your inspiration? Ha-ha-ha-**ha**! Ridiculous!'*

"In-voke-your-**presence!**" G. sang in the same notes as Beethoven's Fifth.

52

"Damn," he continued in the same stream-of-consciousness style, *"of all the twenty-four primary exercises, I can only remember one of them, and now I find myself just knowing vaguely that it exists . . .*

"What was that one exercise I was able to remember? This is all very embarrassing, I'm sweating from embarrassment . . . but this also reminds me of something . . .

*"Yes, I've heard that the unveiling of the non-phenomenal self generates heat . . . but that can only come as a result of the invocation of presence, which doesn't usually just happen by itself . . . now I feel remorse, and it's all **his** fault.*

"After all, I'm new here; I shouldn't be expected to perform as well as the others; they've all had more practice at this sort of thing and . . ." G.'s narrative came to a stop, and he sat back against the chair, at the same time signaling for the dessert and coffee to be served from the kitchen.

"This is an example of the use of mental and organic momentum for the purpose of self-invocation. It is a method by which we use the force of ordinary life against itself, allowing the momentum to proceed, but changing its form and its effect upon us.

"We are still influenced by the full force of organic life, still under the influence of the momentum of our ordinary habits, but the influence is *applied* . . . to the invocation of presence.

"As a group, review now all exercises as possible remembering factors, generating a list of every little work-trick you know. Do this group review of exercises and remembering factors periodically.

"Even notate methods of which you have only heard and about which you know nothing whatever in the practical sense; they may frustrate you into invocation."

CHAPTER NINE

REMEMBERING TO INVOKE PRESENCE

G. was seated at the dinner table surveying the group with a glance when he noticed R., G.'s favorite kitchen helper, was not at the table. "R., get out of the kitchen!" G. roared. "Come sit with us at the table. You always remain in the kitchen rather than join us at the table. You are always finding things to do in the kitchen so you can stay in there. This is an example of *momentum.*

"However, you do not wish to let this momentum 'carry you through'. You start a task and it is natural to work at the task as if you will finish it, but at a school you must not perform a task just by momentum, the path of least resistance. Learn to break the momentum, and if necessary, do something else.

"Most people remain in a mood just by momentum. They may change posture, climb out of their state, but return to the mood due to momentum."

As R. came out of the kitchen to sit with the group, G. asked, "What formulation would be significant to those who know nothing of the invocation of presence?" G.'s question was met momentarily by silence from the 'dead-pan' faces around the chamber.

"'I am here' and 'I am here now' are not as effective as 'I invoke the presence of my presence into the present'," G. said.

"Is invocation of presence an early preparatory technique for invocation of the Absolute?" M. asked.

"Invocation of presence is not far removed from invocation of the Absolute," G. replied.

"In contemporary western civilization, people seem to miss performing prayer," M. said. "Due to the trend to adopt the path of the search for spiritual awakening according to the many eastern religious traditions, people have been offered what they regard, perhaps even unconsciously, as a strange form of prayer. As a result, there may be people now who actually wish to learn to pray in relation to real ideas."

"Self-invocation is a form of prayer," G. said, "to invoke your own presence, to invoke an angelic presence, or to invoke the Absolute, the same factors are necessary. In addition, another factor – the process of invocation itself – must be reinforced in the same way as a train, which slowly rises from inertness to momentum as it gathers force to accelerate.

"When invoking presence, take advantage of momentum by adding to it; maintain the momentum of invocation.

"You look puzzled, D. Can it be that you are unfamiliar with the idea of momentum? When the engineer starts a choo-choo train moving down the track, does he start the engine and then immediately stop it, allowing the train to roll down the track by itself? Doesn't he add more and more energy to the forward motion of the train by adding velocity to already proceeding velocity?

"When boiling water, do you add heat only at the beginning and then soon afterward turn it off?

"Haven't you noticed in the course of events, during

the last several decades of your life in which you must have realized, even if only by observing another at work, that if hot water is added to hot water, it increases the temperature much more easily than hot water added to cold water, and that if you can find a way to capture and somehow heat the vapor itself, you have an even more efficient accumulation of heat."

"Are you marrying the idea of momentum and invocation?" D. asked.

"Do you wish to also be invited to the reception and later to be a witness in the bridal suite during the obligatory consummation?" G. asked dryly.

"I simply didn't want to let what you said slip by unnoticed," D. replied.

"What do you suppose she means by this?" G. asked.

"To keep an invocation going," K. replied, "how would you, after starting an invocation, keep it going, build on it, take advantage of its momentum to make it either self-maintaining or maintaining by suggestion . . . or is there another more effective way to do this that you have learned about and would like to present to us?"

"Exactly how would you self-invoke?" asked G. "Not more or less, but exactly how?"

"I would use the phrase – 'I hereby invoke the presence of my presence into the present'," K. said, "or if I were ill or in a negative state, I would use the phrase, 'I wish this – meaning my negativity – to be used for the invocation of the presence of my presence into the present'."

"Even more effective," G. replied, "would be to use the negative force to feed the invocation. A slightly more sophisticated invocation would serve this purpose, such as, 'I wish this' . . . referring to the negative force, including such negative forces as the sensations of happiness, ecstasy, nostalgia, pleasure and religion . . . 'to be used to feed the invocation of the presence of my presence into the present.'

"This can even be used later, when you begin to invoke much greater presences than your own. But this is not the real question. Anyone can learn the secrets of invocation, which are not very inaccessible even in ordinary life. The real question is, how do you remember to self-invoke?"

"I set the intention to remember," K. replied.

"You set the intention to remember to invoke yourself, meaning, I suppose, that at some time before your invocations begin for the day, you decide to remember to invoke yourself into the present.

"And using this method, how often do you successfully remember to invoke your presence?" G. asked.

"I tend to remember to invoke my presence more often when I am in a positive state than from a negative state," she replied, "but I haven't any real means of remembering to self-invoke."

"The invocation of presence in a positive state is practically useless," G. commented, "because it neither feeds the invocation nor does it provide any definite indication of a successful invocation, which is to say, the washing away of a negative state in the presence of presence.

"In addition, be very cautious when referring to positive states. The majority of states considered positive in ordinary life are really negative because they depend upon some organic centrum of attention, and also because the emotion is really a sensation, group of sensations, or a definite or indefinite series of sensations.

"The times I have remembered most to invoke presence are times I feel very asleep," D. said, "when I feel heaviness overwhelming me."

"Sleep is a good remembering factor," G. agreed, "and best of all are those feelings engendered in your machine by your remorse when you have forgotten to invoke yourself.

"Forgetfulness, inattention, identification . . . these are the keys to self-invocation. They provide the feeling basis for invocation.

"The self-shame engendered following periods of sleep and inattention can be a very powerful source of force with which to feed your invocations.

"Use these feelings of failure and frustration now, while you can. The day will come when they no longer provide force and you will be compelled to gather around yourself only those who make your life miserable and uncomfortable and who can, because they have not yet lost the impulses of machine-frustration, produce in themselves, without half thinking about it, vast amounts of negative force.

"Unfortunately for them but fortunately for you and for others like yourself – who are compelled to depend upon the negative force of others at the same time that they remain under the influence of the machine – they have no data for self-invocation.

"Someday soon, if you continue your self-invocations regularly, and bathe in the cleansing radiations resulting from self-invocation and the invocations of higher presences than your own, you will find yourself in the same predicament as other vampires.

"You are now learning to depend upon negative force for your invocations.

"But what about the day when you lose your own negativity? When – thanks to the cleansing effects of the radiations emanated from various invoked presences – your centrums are balanced and your strivings and impulses have been reduced to zero, when there is in you no driving force one way or another, that is to say, when you have no axe to grind.

"For the day on which you wake up to find yourself completely impartial to organic life and to the events proceeding within it, you must be prepared.

"A community in which the conditions for continual irritation must be organized.

"The members of the community must be made aware – by law – that they have been invited to participate in an unending process of friction, grinding down, which has the effect useful for you, but painful and perhaps even unbearable for them, thanks to the effects of self-invocation, should they ever seriously undertake the discipline introduced by you, again according to certain laws of the Work, of generating negative force on a scale corresponding to your own invocational necessity without the need for your continual intervention or provocation.

"The fact is, any group of people will provide this friction more or less nonstop under almost any conditions, if they are forced to tolerate one another and accommodate themselves to the annoying habits of others.

"There are those here this evening who have been given data on this subject which would be useful to the entire group," G. said.

"The idea of the use of negative force produced by the ordinary momentum of organic life can provide the majority of your remembering factors, and at the same time also feed your invocations and, by the absence of the negative force, also indicate a successful invocation.

"Just place yourself in my hands . . . live as I do, and accommodate yourself on a minute-by-minute basis to the needs and demands, whether real or imaginary, of those I have intentionally invited to be near me . . . *that* should remind you to invoke your presence!

"Whenever you feel the sensations of negative emotion, without pause to reflect on its significance or your feelings about your negative state, you should use these sensations to help you remember to self-invoke, and with the use of the addition to the ordinary invocational phrase, the invocation itself should remind you to use the negative force to feed the invocation . . .

"But I can think of several reasons other than those I have already mentioned for negative force as a means of continuing the momentum of self-invocation," G. said.

"What reasons?" D. inquired.

"Would you allow me to rob you and your friends of a chance to work?" G. asked. "You should exercise your attention and mentation just a little, or your tail-brain will grow fat and lazy. Of course, if you are a secretary or a typist, this will provide some very nice additional padding for your auspicious behind!"

R. had been about to speak for several moments, and when G. paused, he said, "Once I was about to explode from negative emotion, but I caught it just before the explosion. It was like waves of heat pounding outward from my body. It produced a definite sensation, the same kind you get from the desert sun."

"Suppose you had self-invoked just at that moment?" G. proposed.

"I wish I had," he replied. "I think my state would have provided a vast amount of energy, but at the time I had no data. I didn't know about self-invocation. I'm not sure if it wouldn't carry me away again so completely that I would forget entirely about invocation," he admitted.

"I have at times caught myself, kept myself," P. confided. "I felt what I would call a transformation of sorts, what seemed to be the sensation of something in me being absorbed or eaten by someone or something."

"Did you sense this as something washing through you?" G. queried. "Did you sense heat, a twinge of pain in your chest or a feeling of anxiety? Do you recall experiencing a sensation – what do they call it? – a sensation of longing . . . yearning . . . the sensation of home sickness, the hot hunger, the desire, the urge? All this is useful for invocational force, or you may feed it to Lunar Parasite if it is expressed. Even if not expressed, it will go to some Lunar Parasite if it is not used as force to invoke presence.

"On the other hand, at a *school* when you fall into a negative state, you are trained to invoke presence, and as your presence comes into the present, as it takes root, it will feed itself . . . it will eat the negative force. In this way, you are *feeding your own presence*, your possible evolutionary-angelic-self."

"Why not say, 'I invoke my angelic presence'?" K. asked.

"When you invoke the presence of your angelic self, then you are speaking not from the presence, but from the machine," G. said. "'I invoke the presence of my presence into the present.' Now I am speaking from the source, from the presence – hauling myself down by my own bootstraps."

"Feeding the angelic self with the force of negative emotion . . ." D. began.

"Nurturing and feeding," G. clarified, "the Lunar Parasite is fed by manifested organic emotion, the angelic self by substance resulting from organic emotion used to invoke presence. You have a choice. At the end of the day tote the score. Who has grown the fatter of the two?"

"Does Lunar Parasite get hungrier and hungrier the more the angelic self is fed?" P. asked.

"No need to worry," G. reassured us. "You will not starve the Lunar Parasite for a very long time. Lunar Parasite has a variety of trickeries; it is very crafty in ways that seem harmless. You will be convinced that what you are doing is completely harmless and even useful, as it hovers, chuckling to itself in amusement. Vampirism is very real, not at all just an old wives' tale."

"Sometimes I enter into a situation innocently," D. admitted, "and then observe in myself a certain type of sensation which hints to me that it is Lunar Parasite who is near, yet at first I think whatever I am doing is *not* feeding Lunar Parasite, but then there is a little gnawing sensation. Suddenly I become aware of a subtle sensation as if I could see a tiny light in my brain flicker to indicate that what I am doing is of questionable character."

"Ah yes, the tiny blinking red light in the corner of your brain that reads 'SUCKER'," G. smiled.

R., a professional mechanic, remarked, "I am beginning to see the use of invocation as a tool. It seems as if to invoke is like using a wrench."

"You can use the force of organic emotion as a tool in invocation similar to another tool, the *Stop* exercise," G. said. "These are both invocational tools. Surely you know how to use the *Stop* in an invocation . . .?

"As a group, you have two immediate problems," G. said. "First, consider the question, how do you invoke? Along with this is the related question, how do you invoke *what*?

"Another question is, how can you tell an organic emotion when you see one? Nearly all negative emotions are not identified properly as involuntary organic emotion. You have another label for these organic emotions. Perhaps you think of them as something else. What are the labels you attach to organic emotions?"

"Being happy, being comfortable," R. suggested.

You
Have
A Choice

<u>Lunar Parasite</u> | **<u>Angelic Self</u>**

fed by manifested organic emotion

fed by substance resulting from organic emotion used to invoke presence

*At the end of the day, tote the score.
Who has grown the fatter of the two?*

"Sociable," D. offered.

"Having a good time," P. said.

"Taking a break," M. said.

"Indulgence," T. said.

"Being satisfied with myself, and with other people," D. offered.

The group thought of numerous ways to complete this statement such as, "I am just . . . passing time, giving you some feedback 'for your own good' in a work way, listening to gossip because *they* wanted to talk to someone."

"Evidently *everything* is organic emotion," M. concluded.

"Complete the phrase – It is not opinion – it is just my karma . . . it is just my posture . . . I am just laughing at a joke . . . It is funny; I am just having fun."

"I suppose this is also the case with the display of piety and sanctity," D. said.

"What is *not* negative or organic emotion?" K. asked.

"X., what are you eating?" G. asked.

"Nothing," X. replied.

"What was on your finger?" G. asked.

"I was just licking my finger because I had dipped it accidentally in some of Y.'s (her infant daughter's) food," X. explained.

"What is wrong with that? . . . Nothing," G. chuckled, answering his own question.

"How would you recognize an organic emotion ordinarily identified as something else?" G. asked.

"By trying to break the state?" D. asked.

"States considered exalted are usually some form of organic emotion," G. said. "Some states you consider ordinary – even necessary – you cannot imagine functioning without them; yet, they are also organic emotions.

"For instance, what do you do when you greet someone for the first time? Shake hands, smile.

"Imagine encountering the same person while walking

in a hallway at work six times in the same day. The first encounter would be a very cheerful greeting, perhaps pausing for a short time to chat, depending on your mood at the moment. The second encounter would be a friendly greeting. The third would be a quick superficial acknowledgment. The fourth, a flat exchange of glances. The fifth time you would both make serious and even elaborate efforts to avoid crossing paths.

"However, it is stupid to eliminate organic emotion and negative manifestations from your repertoire, because they serve to help you to invoke presence. Should it ever happen that you no longer can have organic community like this with darlings like yourselves who would never be caught dead in Philadelphia – the city of brotherly love – to provide the necessary negative force for your invocations.

"But there are two additional questions to consider tonight . . . First, how to invoke? Secondly, how to provide the invocation with a continuing momentum?" G. left the chamber to retire for the evening.

CHAPTER TEN

THE ESSENTIALS OF

MOMENTUM OF INVOCATION

"You may have the best exercises in the world available for your work," G. said, "but unless you remember to actually *do* them, just knowing about them is of no evolutionary benefit. In some way we must use our ordinary activities and mechanical attention to produce *remembering factors*. The best tool for this is perhaps thinking by association . . . one thing suggests another."

G. asked M. if she remembered a particular detail from the previous evening's talk. Her response was, "I don't know."

"Then you could ask yourself," G. said, "What do I know? Examine your data absolute until this becomes boring, boring, boring . . . as the FoG, the Face of God, the Patchwork Quilt. No matter what I think I see, the King is naked. But it is so frustrating . . . the frustration of organic emotions reminds me to do what? Invoke presence, walking between raindrops . . .

"Thirty exercises could be suggested by the natural

course of events; simply let one exercise suggest another exercise. Then occasionally you should review to see if you have left out an exercise; perhaps there is one you have forgotten.

"As you are reminded of one exercise, try it. Then hopefully this will remind you of another. In this way your whole day can be filled with self-invocations."

CHAPTER ELEVEN

A ROSE BY ANY OTHER NAME

At an early morning hour, W. stormed into the candle-lit chamber in which G. had been working with some of his more intimate pupils. Standing on the top step, towering over everyone seated in the sunken chamber, W. demanded a meeting of the work-group.

G. jumped up and roared, "Then go to the telephone and call long distance to assemble the entire group from everywhere, all over the world! W. wishes a meeting!" As G. stomped out of the chamber, he shouted over his shoulder, "If you wish to handle this upset, then call the children. Call your mother! Call your father! Call everyone to assemble!"

From her high perch, W. flashed an angry glance downward, scanning the astonished, puzzled faces of those seated around the chamber, before she whirled around and dashed out.

G. returned to the chamber and said, "This is an example of the active presence of W.'s Lunar Parasite. Her sense of drama demands that she wake people up and keep them up through the night to talk with her, to assuage her upset." Then he asked L. to find W., who had fled the house into the darkness.

K. offered to help L. with the search. They returned after looking in all the other buildings and walking around the surrounding grounds. As K. took off her shoes and walked over to warm herself by the fire, she sighed in disgust, "This dramatic scene seems ridiculous, absurd!"

G. glanced at K. and asked, "You wish to work? This is also work."

"Well, I do not think I am 'cut out' for it," K. admitted.

"Well, I do not think I am 'cut out' for it either," G. retorted.

"Consider the idea that the chemical factory produces various chemical reactions under certain psychological conditions. Have you noticed that your body produces a definite odor if you become upset, angry or frightened? With this in mind, if we are serious about work, we should be willing to expose our machine to whatever conditions are necessary for work and to produce the alchemical changes which make us able to work."

"Do you mean we must play through these trivial dramas?" K. asked.

"We must *use* pettiness," G. replied. "Just by the tone of your question, it is obvious that you wish to eliminate these dramas. We use whatever is happening in the same way that one uses the Force in *Jiu Jit Su*, using the momentum of our opponent – in this case, organic conditioning – to overcome the opponent.

"If we are weak in a certain way, particularly if we are suggestible and fall easily under hypnotism, we must find a way to use this for our work. What can we do to eradicate hypnotic urges? Destroy the impulse? This is ordinarily impossible and just the resulting frustration should produce an impressive amount of negative force. In this way, even our automatic mechanical suggestibility can work for our work, even if it is part of our organic conditioning.

"For example, O., who is a professional hypnotist, is

very suggestible himself. He has certain beliefs about hypnotism and wishes to verify them whether they are true or not.

"Although he easily hypnotizes and makes effective suggestions to other people, he studies hypnotism as he understands it and only in one crude form; everything he learns will be transformed from its raw state into something conforming to these fixated beliefs already formed in him.

"Therefore, if you are naturally jealous, find a way to use your jealousy for your work. T., you look puzzled. Have you not heard this idea before? Surely someone can help her to understand this idea of *Jiu-Jit-Su* yoga?"

"You have said before that we can use our weak tendencies such as forgetfulness," M. said, "but the most prominent idea I can remember is that we can use remorse as a source of force for our self-invocations into the present."

"I have heard groups talk about the ideas as if they are something to achieve or accomplish," G. said, "and then when people are given this idea of using remorse for their self-invocation, remorse is transformed into the apparent absence of guilt. They paint guilt the color of remorse. Remorse to them is guilt in disguise."

"But what *is* remorse?" L. asked.

"It has been said that remorse is a sensation to be used as a reminding factor to invoke presence," M. said.

"Yes, remorse is a sensation," G. said.

"Is this what was meant in that song that Parker wrote, 'What a sensation . . .'?" T. asked . . . "but you never told us about this idea when we recorded the song," T. complained as G. chuckled.

"What about the idea that we can use remorse in such a way as to reinforce the habit we have hopefully established of invoking presence during periods of stress, so that at death . . .?" M. asked, her voice trailing off at the end.

"Remorse is of no greater significance than a pair of old shoes," G. said. "If a pair of old shoes were useful for your work, I would send you out to buy some, and remorse is of no greater consequence.

"Remorse is a source of force, the basis of a technical method for candidates to ruthlessly use for their transformation, which can only result from the radiations produced during repeated invocations of presence and the effect of these self-invocations upon the organic machine . . .

"The most frequent complaint about the presence exercise is that one cannot remember to do it, and if you do happen to remember, other problems begin to present themselves . . . to begin with, we should remember to *try* to invoke presence, whether immediately successful or not, invoking presence into the body.

"Self-invocation is a magical activity, whether we like to think of it in this way or not, because we are using an invocation to draw the non-phenomenal parts of ourselves into the present, into our organic bodies . . . the task of the sorcerer is to invoke the source. Ah! There is the tension! The invocation of presence is an *invocation*!

"But if we cannot *remember* to invoke, what difference does it make how much we know about self-invocation? It is useless to us *if we forget*.

"Suppose every invocation of presence is successful, but we only remember to invoke ourselves once or twice a year? This would not be very profitable for our work-business. Such infrequent self-invocations are strictly for the hobbyist. Therefore, what would cause us to remember? Perhaps school conditions, yet school conditions are only a small percentage of your entire experience in this world.

"On the other hand, the most important time to invoke presence is under such conditions as extreme pain, stress, anxiety, upset, nostalgia, sentimentality, hysteria, certainty, security, ecstasy, dieting and death. In other words, during a heavy psychological-emotional experience is when we most need the invocation of presence.

"On your deathbed, as you lie there remembering the

vision of all your deaths, they fall like an avalanche upon this new, most immediate death, but by self-invocation, this passing can be viewed in isolation from all other deaths, studied, used consciously as a portal which can carry you beyond the veil, perhaps even provide the force for ascension onto the cross . . .

"When the Second Adam was ejected from the Garden of Eden, he was torn from the Cross, forced by his suffering to descend, after which he was made to walk the Earth with the lower animals.

"If he is ever to return to the Garden and resume his rightful place as the First Adam, he must voluntarily regain the Cross.

"Original sin is the First Adam's willful descent from the Cross into the slow death of organic life, for which he lost his place in the Garden, *which is the same as the descent from the Cross.*"

"In the same way one birth can be isolated from the vision of all births.

"During these times, we are the most needful of the invocation of presence. And we wish to connect the invocation of presence to the most prevalent factor of this experience. Since emotions are not predictable – they do not always and in everything occur exactly the same – and thoughts are too fluid, just a sequential cadence of associations – obviously we wish to use something certain, which occurs every time, to activate our remembering, to remind us to perform the invocation of presence.

"We choose the sensation *remorse* because every organic activity is directed by the machine and not by our own presence, and therefore carries with it *some* remorse. We may not identify it as remorse, but the sensation will occur, for the sensation of remorse is associated with every negative event."

"You mean associated with *nothing*?" K. smirked.

"This 'nothing' I will tell you about," G. chuckled. "Absolute nothing would attract immediate attention, because it is absent in the midst of presence. However, one thing more sure than death and taxes is that the sensation of remorse will be activated often in the course of ordinary life and especially at the passing of the organic body, whether the attention is rooted in the sensing centrum, the thinking centrum, or the power centrum . . .

"First isolate the sensation of remorse in the course of your daily intensive study of the machine, then identify it under any other name – a rose by any other name will smell as sweet.

"The sensation of remorse comes in a variety of disguises such as triumph, glee, elation or even ecstasy. Some religious groups use guilt to produce remorse, which they call ecstasy. Haitian Voodoo rituals and charismatic Christian rituals, common to the southern United States, use this form of 'voodoo-hysteria' also, to produce miracle cures, ecstasy and twenty dollar bills."

"Is this sensation what prompts some people to break into a house and burglarize it?" J. asked.

"Some teenagers steal cars for the thrill of it . . ." G. replied. "They go to great efforts to break into a car and risk killing themselves while fleeing in a higher speed chase to escape the law, and in so doing, often destroy their relationship with their parents and family. The resulting thrill is actually the sensation of remorse . . . at last, something strong enough for them to feel!

"The sensation of remorse is often misidentified as a pleasant emotion. In the same individual, we will find the sensation of remorse under many different emotional aliases.

"If we examine our emotions, we may find that we seem to have dozens, but in fact, there are no emotions in ordinary man – none whatever. Sets of sensations are given emotional names, yet they are not emotions but actually sensations. These sensations are given names of emotions because they are associated with a psychological game or because an event thought to be emotional may activate recognizable sensations.

"People who frequently feel nauseous often manifest in certain ways labeled as emotional, and we are conditioned to think of sensations as emotions.

"A state-name such as sad, upset, unhappy, or confused would be much more accessible if we were able to see that the stomach is jangled and nauseous."

"Emotional moods are actually very simple sensations," W. said.

G. said, "In contemporary society, there is a certain vanity involved with the prestige of being considered emotional, and if people ever came to realize that they had no emotions whatever, especially the more dramatic . . .

"In the Sufi tradition, the work-term 'negative emotion' is technically defined as a sensation or group of sensations which have been wrongly identified as emotion and have somehow come to be called by an emotional name and venerated as an emotion.

"In a technical definition, the words have been chosen very carefully; for instance, in our tradition, 'called by' means 'invoked'. A negative emotion is actually a sensation."

"Then only higher emotions are real emotions?" W. asked.

"Yes," G. replied. "Real emotions have no sensation, they have *feelings*. Real emotions have no moving centrum reverberations.

"If you had real emotion, there would be no sensations such as what you call 'joy' and 'ecstasy' accompanying it. What you call ecstasy is not emotion but sensation. Furthermore, what you normally call thought is not true thought; it is a moving centrum reverberation, a moving centrum event.

"On the other hand, real, higher mentation does not reverberate in the moving centrum. The passage of real thought produces secondary and tertiary reflexes, which are called ordinary thought, actually sensations. Therefore, unevolved man has never had a thought or emotion in his life, *but he thinks he has.* What he is describing as thought and emotion are, in fact, reverberations of sensation in the moving centrum.

"However, because remorse is present during all negative episodes, which is to say, any event which includes organic sensations, especially anxiety, we can use this powerful ever-present sensation for our work. Anxiety, usually understood to be an emotional state, is a sensation resulting from the intentional or accidental agitation of the nervous system.

"Anxiety produces hypothermia, which is characterized by the temporary lowering of the temperature of the body. This physiological change, in turn, produces symptoms such as shivering, agitation, feelings of impending doom, fear, uncertainty and restless wandering. In some cases, hypothermia can even be the cause of such states as suspicion, paranoia and jealousy.

"Let us examine the Five primary organic strivings which the Tibetans call the *Skandhas* – Pride, Lust, Hate, Envy, Jealousy . . . in other words, the primary negative emotions, and the six lower worlds produced by these strivings . . . anger, hatred, fear, jealousy, lust and insatiable hungers, and karma, which is the accumulated result of the momentum of all organic tendencies.

"Exposure to organic life automatically continues and reverberates even beyond the veil, long after our passage out of the electric-magnetic field of organic life, producing the helpless tendency to take rebirth in organic form.

"Nevertheless, the sensation of remorse is a part of all negative episodes; therefore, remorse should be the primary reminding factor to invoke presence.

"It is advantageous to use the sensation of remorse as a remembering factor, because it is more frequently evoked in the course of ordinary life, much as we prefer to think otherwise, than positive remembering factors, and thus provides more external reminding factors.

"Secondly, the sensation of remorse occurs during stress, when presence is most necessary. When we have invoked presence, we can remember – 'This too shall pass'.

"Thirdly, the invocation of presence is a sure-cure for negative episodes, for presence – when properly invoked – can, *in the moment,* take authority over the machine, the beginning of real will."

CHAPTER TWELVE

STEP BY STEP METHOD

TO INVOKE PRESENCE

"Did I ever give you a step-by-step method to invoke presence?" G. asked.

"You gave us the mantrum 'I wish this to be used to invoke the presence of my presence into the present'," T. said.

"A mantrum is useless without a step-by-step method to invoke presence," G. said. "'I wish to invoke the presence of my presence into the present' is useless by itself. For the invocation of presence, there must be a *basis*, a foundation. It does not just happen by itself. Something must serve to *feed* the invocation.

"First, *'I wish'* . . . I establish firmly that the 'I' refers to the source of my attention and not to the machine 'I'.

"Second, there must always be a *'this'* in the invocation, which refers to something upon which the invocation can feed. I use my sensing apparatus to illuminate, to keep track of what I refer to as *'this'* in my self-invocation. Using my sensing apparatus like a theatrical 'follow-spot', I follow, define, encapsulate and reveal this feeding substance to one part of my continuous attention so that *at any moment during the invocation,* I am aware with my sensing apparatus what the word *'this'* refers to.

"*'To be used'* . . . the silent sounding of these words, I know that when I say *used,* I am offering up the feeding substance in the same way that I would place food at an altar, not in the contemporary tradition in which the food is hastily removed for use in the kitchen, but in the ancient sense in which the priest or priestess consumed the food only during the descent of the invoked presence.

"*'To invoke'* . . . with my sensing apparatus, I mentally form a funnel with myself at the bottom, drawing the presence down to myself in a mental posture resembling the Movements posture 4-2.

"*'The presence of my presence'* . . . why not just my presence? Because it is not just my presence which is detected by my sensing apparatus. I wish to invoke not only my presence, but the *feelable presence* of my presence, the tangible *atmosphere*, its radiations, emanations and mood, which is to say, the *nimbus*, or *Aura*, which descends upon me extending outward in all directions like a living, pulsing sphere of light.

"*'Into the present'* . . . but what do I mean by the present? Rapidly, just for a moment, I take stock of my surroundings – approximate time of day, weather, temperature of the atmosphere, light conditions, sounds, smells, sensations, skin temperature, the location and posture of the body . . .

"Now I put it all together mentally reviewing what each phrase means as it is silently sounded inwardly. As I mentally sound these words, I make certain I can hear them as if I were actually speaking, sometimes even startling myself with the nearness and reverberation of this inner voice. If necessary, I sound each word separately, allowing its reverberation to diminish somewhat before sounding the next word or phrase.

"Afterward, I pause very quietly like a bow-hunter at a

pool waiting for game. I watch and listen with my sensing apparatus. I 'test the atmosphere' looking for any obvious signs that my presence has descended taking particular note to see whether the *'this'* referred to in the invocation has been or is being eaten – absorbed.

"Then I check for a washing sensation descending over and through my organic self-removing – feeding upon – any negative state proceeding at the moment. I then check for subtle alterations in vision, hearing, sensing, smell, taste – all of which should be heightened to some degree however small or large.

"I then ask myself, after several moments have passed, whether my invocation had been successful. And if not, I gather my resources and attention almost tangibly as if gathering great wads of raw cotton in a heap around my body, perhaps as high as my chest, and I try again this time perhaps a little more carefully, more firmly, perhaps more invitingly, even seductively or demandingly or impartially in much the same way that I might try different tonalities of invitation with another person until something worked, realizing that the same intonation will not work every time and seldom works twice in a row.

"If I think of the presence as a person with whom I am intimate, I quickly realize that I cannot order it about even though it is to my own non-phenomenal self that I am speaking. Someday however, my presence will have the habit to descend and it will need no coaxing.

"Periodically, I review to myself in detail the full list of indicators, indicating the presence of presence. I also periodically review possible offerings at the altar of self-invocation – food, dance, manual labor, remorse, pain, illness, inattention, clumsiness, carelessness, argument, frustration and its twin brother, impatience as they walk merrily hand in hand. Even the smallest activity, such as passing through a doorway, can sometimes be used to feed an invocation, although nothing beats a royal flush, whatever that may mean to you.

"If, as often happens, I am unable to arouse the necessary negativity in myself, I bitch, squabble and roar at others who only too willingly oblige with enough food to glut an army of presence in any given moment of the day.

"In many cases, it is necessary to actually provoke this; otherwise, in the atmosphere of presence, which is to say, within its sphere of influence, a more or less perpetual state of self-calm would prevail, except of course under school conditions, an exact set of conditions which make it possible for all this to occur without the necessity for personal intervention, that is to say, an automatically proceeding and self-arising by mechanical momentum, astral heel which finds and crushes under foot any corn that happens to be in the neighborhood."

To the Reader:

The intention of this book is not to provide final answers to all the questions which face a voyager cast adrift in the macro-dimensions; no book can have such a pretense. It can, however, stimulate and nourish the questioning process in which real questions are always followed by still further questions.

Other books by E.J. Gold, and materials in other media – including video and audio downloads, Facebook pages, YouTube videos and interactive training games – may provide answers to questions which will inevitably develop from this material. Those of you who wish to work with this information will find these resources valuable and the innovation of full 3-D simulations of Bardo spaces an exciting development for all of us who pursue this path.

If you feel an urgency to your questions and are prepared to work in a serious way, ongoing training is perhaps the solution for you. You are therefore invited to formulate your questions by writing, emailing, phoning or attending a Zoom workshop.

IDHHB

PO Box 370

Nevada City, Ca. 95959

Phone: 1-800-869-0658 or 530-271-2239

Also visit our websites, Facebook Pages, YouTube Channels and live streaming events.

www.idhhb.com

www.gatewaysbooksandtapes.com

https://www.facebook.com/groups/ProsperityPath

https://www.facebook.com/gorebagg

https://www.youtube.com/c/ejgoldguru

https://livestream.com/gorebaggtv

Art As T'ai Chi
Art As Healing

"Art is a profoundly effective tool for transformation and shamanic skill building. This is all in addition to the well known benefits to brain function, healing, and more."
E.J. Gold

Definitely check out the instructional dvds.
www.idhhb.com/materials/art/

Attention Power

"There are two things you can truly call your own: Attention and Presence" -- *E.J. Gold*

If you don't have Attention Power(tm) and you want to build both memory and attention in a BIG way, you've come to the right place!

- **Attentiasizer**
  Buff up your continuous attention.

- **ORB**
  Works with applied attention, split attention, and threaded attention.

- **P.L.S.**
  Works with focusing attention, exercising roaming attention, and holding attention.

- **Popcorn Exercise**
  Works with infused whole-body attention.

- **Zen Basics**

  Will cleanse and strengthen your attention.

- **Apperception**
  Exercise your attention used in appreception.

Visit: www.attentionpower.com/

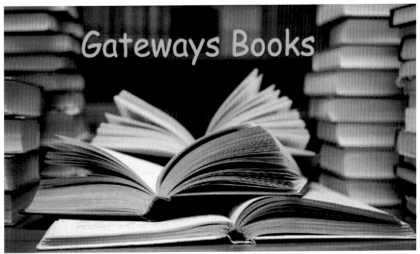

All of Gateways titles share one thing in common — each title is directed to helping seekers on the path.

Since 1971 Gateways has offered books on consciousness, metaphysics, inner work, the Fourth Way, transpersonal psychology, spiritual gaming, music, art, hospice service, attention training, and classic transformational literature.

Gateways' authors include: E.J. Gold, Claudio Naranjo, Robert deRopp, Reshad Feild, John Lilly, Zalman Schachter, Michael Hutchison, Grant Abrams, Claude Needham, Patricia Elizabeth, Grant Abrams, Lee and Glenn Perry, OM C. Parkin, Grace Kelly Rivera and Barbara Haynes.

Visit: www.gatewaysbooksandtapes.com/books/

Brane-Power Technology

Quantum Crystal Radio Technology serving the evolution of humanity. Assisting human growth, awakening and conscious living.

The SuperBeacon™ is primarily a focus point for your psychic-intuitive energies, a crossroad through which very subtle energies pass and are brought into harmonic relationship with one another through a coupling factor of sensitivity & selectivity.

Find the Super Beacon, Zone Box, inductions and other Brane-Power Technology at

www.yoyodyneindustries.com

Brane-Power Amulets

Brane-Power amulets help you gain access to your alpha, delta and theta brain wave states. They assist you in having a better, more creative, intuitional life with easier access to psychic abilities and inner harmony. There are over fifty amulets to choose from at:

www.brane-power.com

Jewelry As a Doorway To The Work

"It really is all about the moves, not about the product. Keep that in mind as you work with the wire and embossing work. It's all a dance. The whole universe is one writhing ball of dance and song." *E.J. Gold*

Visit: www.youtube.com/c/ejgoldguru to view instructional jewelry videos.

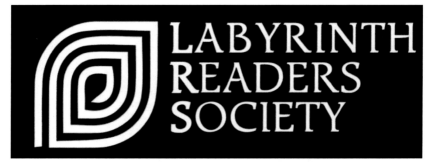

LABYRINTH READERS SOCIETY

Who can be a Labyrinth Reader?

Anyone with a sincere wish to be of service to others can be a Labyrinth Reader. To help you develop your skills and learn the art of being a Labyrinth Reader, the LRS offers courses and training online and throughout the world.

The LRS services and resources are designed to accompany your current beliefs and practices. These techniques and tools can be a powerful addition to your existing spiritual work. We welcome people from all traditions, cultures, and backgrounds. A willingness to be of service and a dedication to compassion is what unites Labyrinth Readers, and is all that's required to get started providing caring service to those in need.

The Labyrinth Readers Society was founded in 1974 to maintain the craft of guiding the individual through the state of Transit between death and rebirth.

For more information visit:

www.facebook.com/LabyrinthReadersSociety
www:labyrinthreaderssociety.com

FAXL MUSIC

"Through the use of sound, specifically variation in rhythmic structures, chord clash and subtractive frequencies, the velocity of the essential self moving through the lifetime (visualized as a tunnel) can be altered. This has the effect of disengaging the essential self from its hypnotic identification with the human biological machine." *E.J. Gold*

Visit: www.faxlmusic.bandcamp.com/music

www.onlythebestcds.com/

Quantum Magic Videos
Prosperity Path GODD Orbs

"The main thing that Quantum Magic Videos (QMV) is doing is empowering people to be able to help themselves or another. It's about the empowerment of each individual to contribute, at whatever level they want, to the well-being of another. That's compassion in action. It's all about how I, as an individual, can be of service to someone in need. Someone that I happen to come across either in the forum, family, or a friend." - User comments

The QMV technology is simple -- that's by design -- to make it accessible to all that wish to use it.

Visit: www.youtube.com/c/QuantumMagicVideos/videos

Prosperity Path is a collection of video game orbs (levels) designed to coach you through a mindful training process that will cleanse your karma and attend to a multitude of life problems.

Visit: www.urthgame.com/

talk of the month

IDHHB brings you talks by E.J. Gold, Claudio Naranjo, Lee Lozowick, John C. Lilly, Zalman Schachter-Shalomi and others, in audio and written form.

These published talks are from the late 1960s through the present covering topics including personal transformation, spiritual life, the Fourth Way, Alchemy, Angels, Attention, Death & Dying, Bardo Training, the Great Work, Healing, Invocation, Metaphysics, the Man on the Cross, Reincarnation, Shamanism, Practical Work on Self, Work Traditions, Gaming and others.

The TalkCDs (also available as a download) are remastered from the original cassettes. They will give you a very real glimpse into the moment by moment transmission of the Teaching.

Visit: www.talkofthemonth.com/

Zen Basics

A tool to bring sanity back into your world.

The primary purpose for Zen Basics is the training of your attention.

You'll be happy to know that Zen Basics will also:

exercise your decision making
expose your own mental inner workings
throw a monkey wrench in the zombie habits.
help you step away from automaticity
dismantle control mechanisms

Zen Basics is an attention trainer for the essential self. Specially designed to work with the higher attention.

The Zen Basics App contains everything you need to get started with Zen Basics Meditation.

Visit ZenBasics.com and do the Zen Basics Simple Practice FREE.

Visit: www.zenbasics.com/